PROGRESS FOR THE POOR

Progress for the Poor

LANE KENWORTHY

OXFORD
UNIVERSITY PRESS

OXFORD

UNIVERSITY PRESS

Great Clarendon Street, Oxford OX2 6DP

Oxford University Press is a department of the University of Oxford.
It furthers the University's objective of excellence in research, scholarship,
and education by publishing worldwide in

Oxford New York

Auckland Cape Town Dar es Salaam Hong Kong Karachi
Kuala Lumpur Madrid Melbourne Mexico City Nairobi
New Delhi Shanghai Taipei Toronto

With offices in

Argentina Austria Brazil Chile Czech Republic France Greece
Guatemala Hungary Italy Japan Poland Portugal Singapore
South Korea Switzerland Thailand Turkey Ukraine Vietnam

Oxford is a registered trade mark of Oxford University Press
in the UK and in certain other countries

Published in the United States
by Oxford University Press Inc., New York

British Library Cataloguing in Publication Data

Data available

Library of Congress Cataloging in Publication Data

Data available

Typeset by SPI Publisher Services, Pondicherry, India
Printed in Great Britain
on acid-free paper by
MPG Books Group, Bodmin and King's Lynn

ISBN 978-0-19-959152-7

1 3 5 7 9 10 8 6 4 2

*For Alex Hicks, Leon Lindberg, Joel Rogers, Wolfgang Streeck,
Jeff Weintraub, and Erik Wright—generous teachers
and mentors, sterling exemplars*

Contents

1

Raise the Floor

One of the principal goals of antipoverty efforts should be to improve the absolute living standards of the least well-off. My aim in this book is to enhance our understanding of how to do that.

ABSOLUTE IMPROVEMENT

Improvement in absolute living standards has several components, each of which is contentious. Begin with absolute improvement. The inspiration comes in part from John Rawls. In *A Theory of Justice*, Rawls asks what distribution of income and wealth is fairest.[1] Because luck plays a large role in determining our abilities, preferences, motivations, and circumstances, Rawls concludes that an equal distribution is fairest. He argues, however, that a rise in inequality is acceptable if it is to the absolute benefit of the least well-off. In this way, Rawls attaches substantial ethical weight to absolute improvement for the poor. In my view he is right to do so.[2]

Why is *improvement* important? Experimental research has found that many people believe justice entails a floor for living standards, below which no one should fall, but not necessarily a rising floor.[3] I don't think policy makers should share this view. In a rich and growing economy, it is difficult to justify stagnant living standards for those at the bottom. As an economy grows, our view about the appropriate floor will tend to be revised upward. This suggests that we favor not simply a satisfactory level of living standards for the poor, but improvement over time.

An additional reason for favoring rising living standards comes from Benjamin Friedman's argument about psychological impact of progress. In *The Moral Consequences of Economic Growth*, Friedman concludes that when people view themselves as better off compared to previous generations, they tend to be more tolerant, more generous, more committed to democracy and good government, and more participatory.[4]

If progress makes sense, why should our goal be *absolute* progress? Most research on poverty in affluent nations uses a "relative" poverty measure. Analysts typically set the poverty line at 50 or 60 percent of the median income within each country. This also is the type of measure used by the European Union in calculating poverty rates.

There are two principal rationales for use of a relative measure of poverty.[5] First, poverty refers to a level of resources insufficient to achieve a minimally acceptable standard of living. Once societies move past subsistence level, it becomes difficult to identify a "minimally acceptable" standard of living in a non-arbitrary way. Hence, as a practical matter it seems sensible to define poverty as relative to what is typical in a given country at a given point in time. Second, proponents of a relative measure suggest that people tend to experience poverty as relative; they gauge their living standards by comparison with what is typical in their own society.

A relative poverty measure has an important drawback, however. It is essentially a measure of inequality in the bottom half of the income distribution. As such, when we assess change over time it can yield a problematic conclusion: the poverty rate may increase even if the absolute incomes of those at the bottom grow.[6] This happens because the median income increases, which causes the relative poverty line to rise, which results in a larger number of people falling under the line. A striking illustration is Ireland, where relative poverty increased between the mid-1980s and the mid-2000s despite significant improvement in the incomes and material well-being of low-end households.[7]

If the absolute incomes or living standards of the poor grow less rapidly than those of households in the middle, that is worth highlighting. It tells us that inequality has increased, and possibly social exclusion as well. But in my view it is not helpful to refer to this as a rise in poverty.

LIVING STANDARDS, INCOMES, MATERIAL WELL-BEING

Is income a useful indicator of living standards? Poverty researchers and government agencies have long relied on income in gauging the living standards of the poor. Income is a resource that allows households to acquire the sorts of things—food, housing, medical care, transportation, and so on—that are needed for a minimally decent standard of living. Income also is comparatively easy to measure.

Yet as an indicator of resources, income has some important drawbacks.[8] It usually is measured over a single year. In any given year the incomes of some surveyed households will be atypical, due to illness, temporary unemployment, an unusually generous bonus, overtime work, or other reasons. For these households, single-year income will overstate or understate true income. Income measures seldom include the value of government services and in-kind benefits. Some low-income households have assets (savings, an owned home) and/or access to credit that enhances their ability to consume, in which case even accurately reported income will understate financial resources. Some low-income households have debt, the financing of which reduces consumption ability. Finally, survey respondents in low-income households tend to underreport income.

Given income's deficiencies as an indicator of material well-being, we might do better to instead examine direct indicators, such as whether people have decent food, housing conditions, medical care, clothing, and transportation. In most rich countries one or more nationally representative surveys now includes questions about these and other indicators of living standards. Unfortunately, these questions are relatively new, so we do not yet have a good sense of how the material well-being of low-end households has or has not changed over time. For the moment, income remains the most useful measure for assessing progress.

PROGRESS FOR THE POOR

There are a number of alternative, though by no means antithetical, visions of what antipoverty policy should aim to achieve: capabilities,[9] opportunity, reciprocity, social inclusion, community, subjective well-being, and others. My intention is not to convince you that improvement in the living standards of the poor is more important than these. Nor am I suggesting that political parties and politicians should put this issue front and center in their election campaigns. A commitment to progress for the poor might or might not be a vote-getter.

Instead, my goal here is simply to lay out the principle that guides the chapters to come. I believe a key concern of policy makers should be to enhance the living standards of the least well-off. This book is about how to do that.

I draw from the experiences of twenty affluent nations over the three decades since the 1970s. These experiences offer valuable lessons, some of which contradict current thinking. As I write, the world's rich countries are emerging from their deepest economic downturn since the 1930s. This follows a period of several decades in which incomes at the bottom of the distribution increased at a very slow pace in some of them. These developments highlight both the importance of boosting the living standards of the poor and the magnitude of the challenge facing policy makers and other economic actors. By improving our understanding of how and why things played out as they did in the 1980s, 1990s, and 2000s, this book aims to help them meet that challenge.

2

Growth Is Good for the Poor, If Social Policy Passes It On

"Growth is good for the poor" proclaimed an influential study prepared for the World Bank in the early 2000s. The study's authors, David Dollar and Aart Kraay, concluded that "Growth on average benefits the poor as much as anyone else in society, so standard growth-enhancing policies should be at the center of any poverty-reduction strategy."[1] More recently, Dani Rodrik opened his book on development strategy, *One Economics, Many Recipes*, by stating matter-of-factly that "Economic growth is the most powerful instrument for reducing poverty. . . . Historically nothing has worked better than economic growth in enabling societies to improve the life chances of their members, including those at the very bottom."[2] These conclusions refer to developing nations. For those countries the notion that economic growth is the key to improving incomes among the least well-off is now widely shared.[3]

Is it true in affluent countries too? Does economic growth tend to significantly boost the incomes of low-end households? It might. An alternative possibility, though, is that the poverty-reducing impact of economic growth diminishes as nations get richer, with less of the growth trickling down to the poor in the form of new jobs and higher wages.

What does the evidence tell us? In comparative studies of affluent nations, the dominant conceptualization of poverty is a relative one. Income growth for the least well-off is assessed relative to income growth in the middle of the distribution. A host of studies have found that when measured in this relative manner, the incomes of the poor do not tend to improve much, if at all, when the economy grows.[4] For the

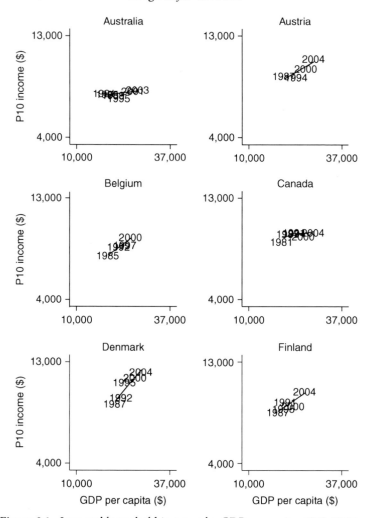

Figure 2.1. Low-end household incomes by GDP per capita, 1979–2007

Note: P10 = tenth percentile of the size-adjusted household income distribution. Incomes are posttransfer-posttax. Incomes and GDP per capita are adjusted for inflation and converted to U.S. dollars using purchasing power parities. GDP per capita is measured as an average over t−5 to t. For data definitions and sources, see the appendix.

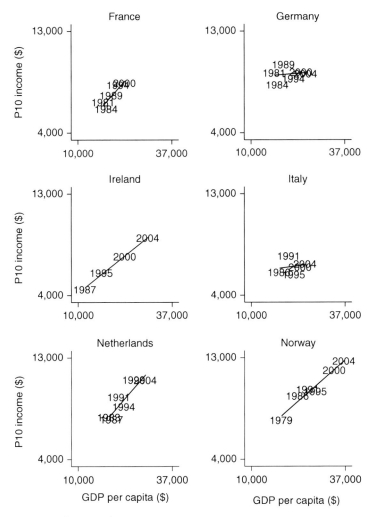

Figure 2.1. Continued

reasons I laid out in Chapter 1, however, my interest is in how much incomes of the least well-off improve in an *absolute* sense.

While various researchers have examined the effect of growth on the absolute incomes of the poor in individual countries, there has been hardly any systematic comparative analysis.[5] As we will see, a comparative approach yields a key insight.

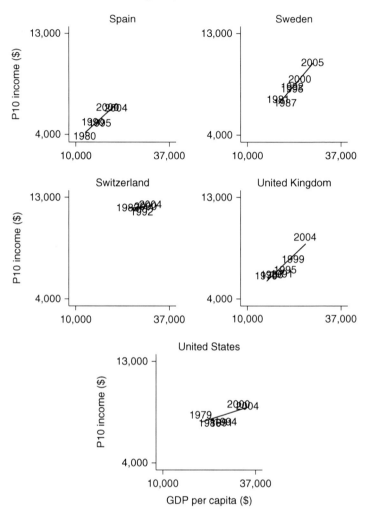

Figure 2.1. Continued

GROWTH IS GOOD FOR THE POOR

Figure 2.1 shows the relationship between low-end household incomes and GDP per capita over time. Data are available for seventeen countries: Australia, Austria, Belgium, Canada, Denmark, Finland, France, Germany, Ireland, Italy, the Netherlands, Norway, Spain,

Sweden, Switzerland, the United Kingdom, and the United States. There is one chart for each country. The period is 1979–2007, though the actual years vary depending on the country. I use the tenth percentile of the income distribution to represent the poor.[6] Tenth-percentile household income is on the vertical axes. GDP per capita is on the horizontal axes. The data points are years.

The income data are from the Luxembourg Income Study (LIS), the best database for comparing incomes in affluent nations.[7] The income measure includes money from earnings, government transfers, and various other sources, with taxes subtracted. For each country the incomes are adjusted for inflation and converted to a common currency (U.S. dollars) using purchasing power parities (PPPs). I also adjust the incomes for household size.[8]

Economic growth has tended to be good for the poor. In most of the countries, the real income level of low-end households is positively associated with GDP per capita over time. On average, an increase of $10,000 in per capita GDP is associated with a rise of about $3,000 in income for a tenth-percentile household with a single person and $6,000 for a household with four persons.

. . . IF SOCIAL POLICY PASSES IT ON

But the degree to which economic growth boosts the incomes of low-end households has varied significantly across these countries. In some nations, tenth-percentile incomes have risen more or less in lockstep with per capita GDP, as indicated by a regression line in Figure 2.1 with a strong positive slope. In others, though, the line is relatively flat, indicating little or no rise in tenth-percentile incomes. Why is that?

The difference across the countries is not due to differences in economic growth. GDP per capita rose in all of these nations. The question is why that produced varying amounts of improvement in the incomes of poor households.

Economic growth is assumed to trickle down to the poor via earnings. As the economy grows, poor households get more jobs, work more hours, and/or receive higher wages. Is that what has happened in these countries since the 1970s?

Using the LIS data, I calculate average levels of the three main sources of income—earnings, other (non-earnings) market income,

Progress for the Poor

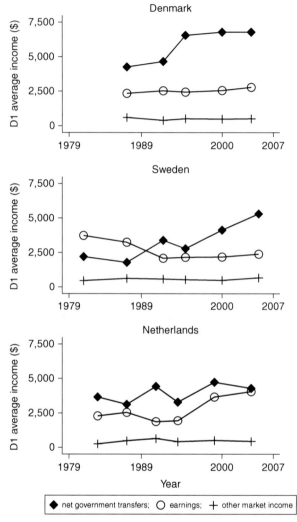

Figure 2.2. Average earnings, other market income, and net government transfers in bottom-income-decile households

Note: The data are averages for size-adjusted income among households in the bottom decile (d1) of the posttransfer-posttax income distribution. Author's calculations using Luxembourg Income Study data. See the text for further discussion.

and net government transfers (transfers received minus taxes paid)—among households in the bottom decile of the posttransfer-posttax income distribution. Figure 2.2 shows the over-time patterns in the

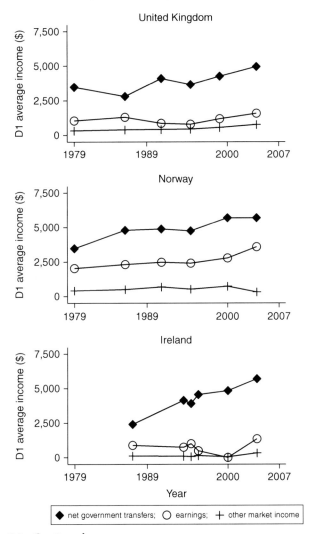

Figure 2.2. Continued

twelve nations for which this calculation is possible.[9] The countries are ordered by the strength of the relationship between per capita GDP and low-end incomes in the charts in Figure 2.1.

In almost all of these countries the earnings of low-end households increased little, if at all, over time. The same is true of other market

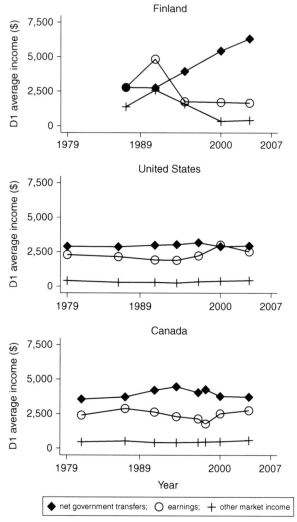

Figure 2.2. Continued

income. It is increases in net government transfers that tended to drive increases in incomes.[10]

In Sweden, Denmark, Norway, the Netherlands, and Finland, net transfers received by low-end households increased significantly between 1979 and 2007.[11] Average earnings were flat in Denmark, while in Sweden and Finland they declined sharply during those countries' deep recessions in the early 1990s. In each of these three countries,

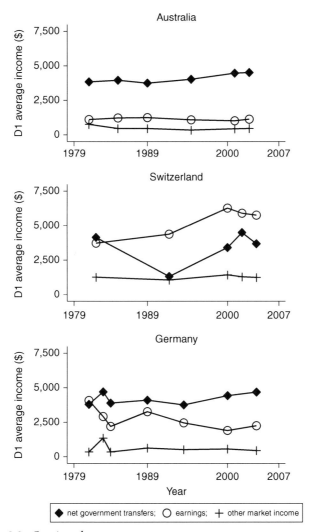

Figure 2.2. Continued

though, the rise in government transfers and/or reduction in taxes was large enough to more than compensate for the stagnation or decline in earnings. In Norway and the Netherlands, earnings rose in the late 1990s and/or early 2000s. In Norway the rise in transfers nevertheless was the principal source of increase in disposable incomes, whereas in the Netherlands net transfers and earnings contributed about equally.

At first glance, developments in Ireland appear similar to those in Sweden, Denmark, and Finland, with net transfers rising while earnings stayed constant or declined. This, however, hides an important part of the story. The composition of the bottom income decile shifted over time in Ireland. Employment and earnings increased sharply in households with working-age heads, enabling some that formerly were at the low end of the income distribution to move up. As a result, the bottom decile came to consist more and more of elderly households. Their incomes rose too, as pension benefits were increased, but not as rapidly as the earnings of working-age households.

In the United Kingdom, the period from 1979 to 1995 saw no change in transfers and a slight drop in earnings. From 1995 to 2005 the story was different: earnings increased slightly, but more important was a large rise in net government transfers, which resulted in a sizeable increase in low-end incomes.[12]

In the United States, economic growth produced virtually no improvement in low-end household incomes from 1979 to 1995 or from 2000 to 2005. In these years both earnings and transfers were flat. The only period in which growth successfully trickled down was the late 1990s. During those years increases in employment and in wage levels at the bottom of the distribution produced a rise in earnings among bottom-decile households. Government transfers stayed constant, with an increase in the Earned Income Tax Credit offsetting reductions in social assistance payments.[13] Developments in the United States are explored in greater detail in Chapter 3.

In Canada, Australia, and Germany, earnings among bottom-decile households were flat throughout the period. So too were net government transfers received by these households. As a result, economic growth produced very little change in low-end household incomes.[14] In Switzerland the result was the same, but due to a rise in earnings coupled with a decline in transfers. Germany, we should remember, has an excuse: it absorbed a poor country (the former East) in the middle of this period.[15]

It is not surprising that government transfers are the main source of rising incomes in low-end households. In most of these countries, 20–35 percent of households have no earnings, and some of those households are in the bottom decile of the income distribution. As of the early to mid-2000s, the share of bottom-income-decile households with zero earnings ranged from 40 percent in Finland and

Norway to 75–80 percent in Ireland and Belgium.[16] Some of these are households with working-age adults whose chief income source is government benefits such as social assistance or unemployment, sickness, or disability compensation. Others are elderly households with savings and pensions as the main source of income.[17]

Should we bemoan the fact that earnings have played so small a role as a source of trickle down to bottom-decile households? Employment can and should be a key part of strategies for reducing poverty and inequality and for shoring up the welfare state.[18] And if we look higher in the income distribution, in the second and third deciles, earnings do play more of a role.

But my focus here is on the bottom decile of households. It is a large group—roughly 90 million people across the twenty countries I examine in this book. For this bottom 10 percent there are limits to what employment can achieve. In all of these countries, 5 percent or more of working-age households have no employed adult.[19] Some people have psychological, cognitive, or physical conditions that limit their earnings capability. Others are constrained by family circumstances. At any given point in time some will be out of work due to structural or cyclical unemployment. And in all rich countries a large and growing number of households are headed by retirees. For these reasons, it probably is unrealistic to expect employment to be the solution for many bottom-decile households.[20]

Where net government transfers increased, this was underwritten by economic growth. None of these countries significantly raised the share of GDP going to transfers during this period.[21] Economic growth allowed policy makers to boost inflation-adjusted benefit levels for transfer programs, which increased the incomes of benefit recipients. With GDP rising, government social transfers as a share of GDP tended to remain more or less constant. In some countries the rise in net transfers was achieved in part by reduction of taxes for low-income households. Governments in countries as diverse as the United Kingdom, Ireland, the Netherlands, and Sweden have boosted the incomes of the least well-off via alterations in taxation over the past generation.

Still, whether or not to pass on the fruits of economic growth is a policy choice, and some countries chose to pass on more than others. We can see this in the charts in Figure 2.2. Though rising incomes for the poor in recent decades have not been a function of policy makers increasing the share of GDP that goes to government transfers, they *have* hinged on whether or not net transfers grow in concert with the economy.

Why, then, did some countries keep transfers in line with per capita GDP while others did not? The countries with little rise in low-end incomes, due to little rise in net transfers received by low-end households, are Australia, Canada, Germany, Italy, Switzerland, the United Kingdom (aside from 1995–2005), and the United States (except 1995–2000). Apart from Germany, these nations tend to be comparatively low in social policy generosity.[22] Countries with high *levels* of social policy generosity have tended to pass on more of the gains from economic growth to low-end households via *increases* in transfers.

There is nothing automatic about this. In fact, we might expect policy makers in high-generosity countries to have passed along less of those gains, given that transfers already were generous. Similarly, we might predict that policy makers in low-generosity nations would have decided to pass on more, in order to bring their social policy generosity into line with that of their high-generosity counterparts. But that has not happened. On the contrary, policy makers in high-generosity nations have been more likely to pass on economic growth's gains.[23] In those countries the generosity of transfer programs has tended to be tied to economic progress—sometimes explicitly, with benefit levels indexed to average earnings, and in other instances via periodic policy updates. In all likelihood the factors that have produced higher levels of social policy generosity in these countries—strong labor, successful left parties, conducive political institutions, and perhaps others—also make them more likely to increase net transfers as the economy grows.

CONCLUSION

Since the 1970s most of the world's rich nations have not significantly increased the share of their GDP that goes to transfers for the poor. They could have done so, and some may elect to do so in the future. But there are limits to this strategy for boosting the incomes of low-end households. If the pie does not increase in size, a country can redistribute until everyone has an equal slice but then no further improvement in absolute incomes will be possible. For the incomes of the poor to rise, we need economic growth.

Economic growth has been good for the poor in the world's rich nations over the past generation. But not always. Some countries—Australia, Canada, Germany, Italy, Switzerland, the United Kingdom (1980–95), and the United States (1980–95 and 2000–5)—have experienced lengthy periods of economic growth with little or no rise in the incomes of low-end households. When growth has trickled down to the poor, government transfers have been the principal conduit. It is in countries that have increased transfers in concert with per capita GDP that the incomes of the poor have tended to rise.

3

How Trickle Down Can Fail: The U.S. Case

Lane Kenworthy and Keith Bentele

The experiences of the world's rich countries since the 1970s, examined in Chapter 2, suggest that economic growth boosts incomes for poor households. Rising tides have tended to lift all boats. Yet this tendency has been just that: a tendency. Economic growth has made rising low-end incomes more likely, but several countries, and particular periods in other countries, are notable exceptions. They experienced growing per capita GDP but little or no improvement in the incomes of low-end households.

As we saw in Chapter 2, the failure of some governments to increase public transfers as the economy grows is a key part of the reason. But why didn't more economic growth reach the poor in the form of rising market incomes? In this chapter we explore the relationship between economic growth and the market incomes of low-end households in one of the countries with less generous social policy: the United States. In addition to its substantive importance as the largest and most economically powerful affluent nation, the United States has several features that make it a useful case for analysis. First, data from the annual Current Population Survey (CPS) allow us to investigate the main routes through which economic growth is likely to directly benefit the poor: employment hours and hourly wage levels. Second, the degree of trickle down in the United States has varied over time. During the 1979–89 and 2000–7 business cycles economic growth produced no increase in the market incomes of low-end households, while in the 1989–2000 business cycle those incomes did rise, albeit modestly. Third, we can utilize variation across the fifty American states for analytical leverage.

Using state-level data for the years 1979–2007, we examine the impact of economic growth on tenth-percentile (P10) pretransfer-pretax household incomes and we explore the causal paths through which it operates.

THE PUZZLE

The first chart in Figure 3.1 displays levels of GDP per capita and P10 pretransfer-pretax household income in the United States from 1979 to 2007. Because our focus in this chapter is on market incomes, we include only households with a "head" age 25–59; this excludes most retirees and students. As in Chapter 2, we adjust household incomes for inflation and for household size. The trends differ starkly: GDP per capita grew steadily during this period of nearly three decades, whereas the market incomes of households at the low end of the distribution were stagnant.

The second chart in Figure 3.1 shows the association between per capita gross state product (GSP, the state-level counterpart to gross domestic product) and low-end household incomes in each of the U.S. states. GSP per capita is on the horizontal axis and P10 market income is on the vertical axis. Each line represents the over-time association in a particular state. (Here and throughout, we exclude Alaska.) The data points from which the lines are created are business-cycle peak years: 1979, 1989, 2000, and 2007. In some states we observe the expected positive association, but in many of these the association is not especially strong. Moreover, in quite a few states there is no relationship, and in some the association is negative.

Why has economic growth trickled down to the market incomes of poor households to such a limited extent?

ECONOMIC GROWTH, EMPLOYMENT HOURS,
WAGES, AND MARKET INCOMES

The proceeds of a growing economy can trickle down to the market incomes of the poor via more hours of paid employment and/or

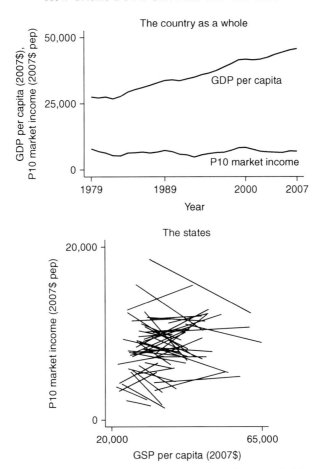

Figure 3.1. GDP or GSP per capita and low-end market household incomes, 1979–2007

Note: P10 = tenth percentile of the working-age household pretransfer-pretax income distribution. Income is adjusted for household size; "pep" = per equivalent person. In the second chart, each line is a regression line estimating the (bivariate) over-time relationship in a particular state. The data points (note shown) are business-cycle peak years: 1979, 1989, 2000, and 2007. Alaska is not included. Horizontal axis is truncated. For data definitions and sources, see the appendix.

higher hourly wages.[1] In Chapter 2 the focus was on the bottom 10 percent, and it turned out that little economic growth reaches this group via labor market trickle down. In this chapter we therefore examine a larger group. With the CPS data we can calculate measures of employment hours and hourly wage rates. For the former, we use the average annual number of hours of employment among working-age households in the bottom quartile of the pretransfer-pretax income distribution. We measure the latter as the tenth percentile of the hourly wage distribution among persons with a paying job. Details for these and all other measures are in the book's appendix.

What has been the impact of economic growth on employment hours and wages? Figure 3.2 displays regression lines for each of the states. Here too we include only business-cycle peak years, as our interest is in progress across business cycles, rather than movement within business cycles.

In the top chart we do not observe the expected association between per capita gross state product and employment hours in low-end households. Most of the lines are flat or negatively sloped, indicating that in most of the states work hours in those households have not tended to rise as the economy grows.

When we turn to the impact of economic growth on low-end wages, displayed in the lower chart in Figure 3.2, the patterns do tend to conform to the trickle-down expectation. In virtually all of the states, as per capita GSP rises so does the tenth-percentile hourly wage level.

Figure 3.3 examines the second step in the causal chain: the effect of employment hours and wage levels on low-end household incomes. The top chart in the figure indicates a very strong positive over-time association between work hours in low-end households and the incomes of such households. As employment hours go up, so too do household incomes. This is true for virtually every state.[2]

The lower chart in Figure 3.3 shows a positive but weaker impact of increases in tenth-percentile wage levels on the market incomes of low-end households. This pattern too holds in many of the states.

Employment hours

Work hours matter a great deal for the incomes of poor households in the United States. Indeed, the charts in Figure 3.3 suggest that employment hours have been a much stronger driver of trends in low-end household incomes than have wage levels. How much stronger? We estimate a pooled time-series cross-section regression, using the data for each of the forty-nine states in the peak business-cycle years of 1979, 1989, 2000, and 2007. This regression includes state

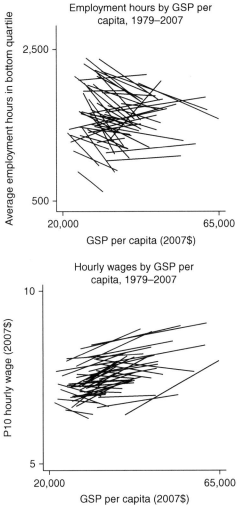

Figure 3.2. Employment hours in low-end households and low-end hourly wages by gross state product per capita, 1979, 1989, 2000, and 2007

Note: See the note to Figure 3.1. Employment hours and market incomes are for households with a "head" age 25–59. Employment hours are calculated as the yearly average among working-age households in the bottom quartile of the income distribution. Chart axes are truncated. For data definitions and sources, see the appendix.

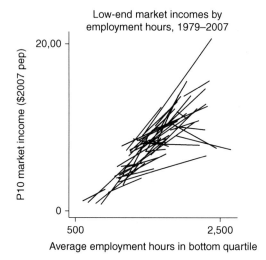

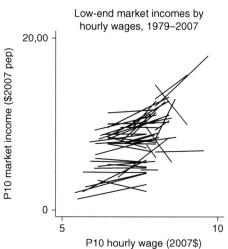

Figure 3.3. Low-end market incomes by employment hours in low-end households and by low-end hourly wages, 1979, 1989, 2000, and 2007

Note: See the notes to Figures 3.1 and 3.2. Employment hours and market incomes are for households with a "head" age 25–59. Horizontal axes are truncated. For data definitions and sources, see the appendix.

dummy variables in order to focus on the over-time patterns within states rather than on the cross-state variation. Hourly wage levels and average employment hours in low-income households are not very strongly correlated with one another, so both can be included as independent variables in the regression.[3] The results suggest that the impact of employment hours has been approximately four times as large as that of wage levels. An increase of four standard deviations—roughly from the low end of the range to the high end—in average employment hours in low-end households is estimated to increase the tenth-percentile household income level by approximately $8,000 (in 2007 dollars per equivalent person). By contrast, an increase of four standard deviations in the tenth-percentile hourly wage is estimated to raise the income of a tenth-percentile household by about $2,000.

But the pattern in the top chart in Figure 3.2 tells us that economic growth has not tended to boost employment hours in low-end households. All of the states experienced economic growth, yet average employment hours among low-end households increased in just nine states. For low-end households, then, the past generation has been one of "jobless growth." Employment has increased among the population as a whole; indeed, the 1980s and 1990s featured a sustained rise in the U.S. employment rate.[4] But that has not translated into more hours of work for the typical household in the bottom quartile of the income distribution.

What explains this lack of increase in employment hours among low-end working-age American households?

One factor is shifts in household composition. Recent decades have witnessed a rise in the share of working-age households with only a single adult. This will tend to reduce work hours in the typical low-end household. Particularly likely to have zero or few hours of employment are single-adult households headed by women. Women are much more likely to care for children in instances of out-of-wedlock birth and divorce, and until the late 1990s they had greater access than men to government financial supports that would enable them to survive without employment.[5]

This means that to gauge the true impact of economic growth on employment hours in low-end households, we need to control for changes in the share of persons in female-headed households. It turns out, however, that doing so does not produce positive associations between economic growth and changes in employment hours in most states. In other words, few of the lines in the top chart in Figure 3.2 become positively sloped.

A second possible contributing factor is changes in educational attainment among less-skilled Americans. The general trend over the past century has been in the direction of greater schooling, but this stalled in the 1970s. Did educational attainment among those at the low end of the labor market decline, perhaps due in part to heightened immigration by individuals with limited schooling? No. Schooling completion among recent cohorts has been stagnant; it has not decreased.[6] Moreover, because the average level of schooling among younger cohorts is higher than among those retiring, their entry into the labor force continues to raise the average educational attainment among working-age Americans.[7]

If changes in household composition and in education do not account for the lack of positive association between economic growth and work hours in low-end households, the next suspect to consider is changes in the number and types of jobs available to the poor.

Is the problem that employment hours in these households were already quite high at the beginning of the period? No. In 1979 the average across the states was 1,540. A typical work year for one person employed full-time year-round is approximately 2,000 hours, so 1,540 leaves a good bit of room for increase. The average rose to 1,590 in 1989 and to 1,660 in 1999 before plummeting to 1,390 in 2007.

Perhaps, then, the problem is lack of job creation. Economic growth can trickle down via employment hours in two ways. First, people who already have a job work more hours. Second, people formerly without any job become employed. The latter happens only if the number of jobs increases.

The top chart in Figure 3.4 shows the over-time association, for the country as a whole, between GDP per capita and the employment rate among those age 25–64. In the growth phases of the 1980s and 1990s business cycles, the employment rate increased at a fairly healthy clip. Indeed, compared to other affluent nations, this employment performance was quite good.[8] And job creation at the low end of the wage distribution was more rapid in the 1980s and 1990s than in the 1960s and 1970s.[9] For the 1980s and 1990s, then, the problem was not economic growth's failure to produce new jobs for Americans at the bottom of the distribution.

The lower chart in Figure 3.4 suggests that the key was what happened during the *downturn* phase of the 1980s and 1990s business

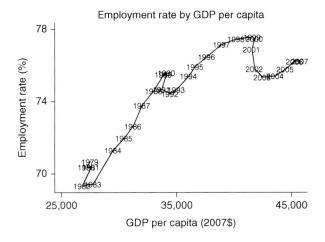

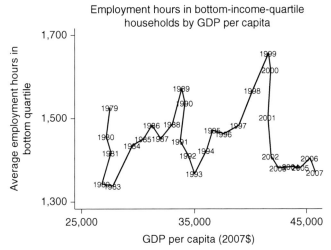

Figure 3.4. Employment rate by GDP per capita and employment hours by GDP per capita, the country as a whole, 1979–2007

Note: See the notes to Figures 3.1 and 3.2. The employment rate in the first chart is for all working-age persons, not just those with low earnings or incomes. Employment hours in the second chart are for bottom-income-quartile households with a "head" age 25–59. Chart axes are truncated. For data definitions and sources, see the appendix.

cycles. That chart shows the over-time association between per capita GDP and average employment hours in working-age households in the bottom quartile of the income distribution. The problem is not that growth failed to boost hours, but rather that recessions dramatically reduced hours. Average employment hours among low-end households increased steadily between 1983 and the peak year of 1989, but they had dropped quite a bit between 1979 and 1983. As a result, not until the final year of the 1980s business cycle, 1989, did they reach and surpass the level of 1979. The 1990s business cycle was similar. Employment hours rose quite sharply between 1993 and 1999–2000, but they had dropped so precipitously between 1989 and 1993 that once again it was not until the very peak of the business cycle that they exceeded the previous cycle's high. In the ensuing downturn they again fell sharply.

The 2000s business cycle was different. Economic growth from 2000 to 2007 was reasonably strong, but it produced no increase in the employment rate. Indeed, the employment rate in 2007 was more than a percentage point lower than it had been in 2000. Average employment hours in bottom-income-quartile households barely budged in the growth phase of this cycle. For this decade, jobless growth is an apt characterization.

Jobless growth, then, is the key to why low-end market incomes were stagnant in the mid-to-late 2000s. In the 1980s, 1990s, and early 2000s, though, the story was the dramatic loss of employment hours during economic recessions. The problem is not that economic growth has failed to help the poor. It has indeed helped. But recessions since the 1970s have been very rough on America's poor, and the benefits of growth have not been sufficient to offset the damage.[10]

The pattern we observe likely rules out another influential hypothesis: that generous social policy is to blame. In this view, government benefits reduce the incentive for Americans with limited skills to take a low-paying, not-very-satisfying job.[11] Economic growth therefore has little impact on work hours. We see in the lower chart in Figure 3.4 that in fact work hours did rise quite sharply during the growth years of the 1980s and 1990s. Ironically, it was in the 2000s, after incentives for employment were significantly enhanced by the 1996 welfare reform, that we see no jump in work hours in response to economic growth. The demographic group that was the focus of welfare reform, poor single mothers with children, did experience a rise in employment hours and consequently in market incomes.[12] However, improvement for this group has not translated into improvement for America's poor overall.[13]

Why did employment hours in low-end working-age households fall so dramatically during these three economic downturns? We are not certain, but the answer seems most likely to center on the high degree of employer discretion and the limited organizational strength of those at the bottom that characterize the American labor market. Employers in the United States are largely free to fire at will, and in the absence of strong unions it is no surprise that those with the most limited skills or with other human capital deficits tend to be vulnerable to dismissal or reduction of work hours during a downturn.

Two other specific features of these recessions are worth noting. The recession of the early 1980s was an especially severe one in terms of employment loss. The Federal Reserve pushed up interest rates to an extremely high level in order to combat inflation, and this produced massive job losses. The recessions of the early 1990s and early 2000s were less severe in this respect, but by then employers had begun to adopt a more cautious approach to adding employment. Downsizing was the strategy du jour.[14] And according to some observers, health-care costs had become a significant deterrent to hiring.[15] Whatever the cause, a cautious orientation toward hiring and adding hours seems to have been especially consequential in the 2000s, as the overall employment rate and employment hours in low-end households remained stuck long after the low point in the business cycle.[16]

Wages

The lack of trickle down over the past several decades has stemmed not only from developments in work hours but also from trends in wages. The lower charts in Figures 3.2 and 3.3 suggest the problem is not so much that wages have failed to respond to economic growth, but rather that they have had limited impact on the incomes of low-end households.[17]

Careful inspection of over-time patterns in individual states suggests a nontrivial degree of correspondence between trends in wages and trends in household incomes. The disjuncture in trends occurs chiefly in two periods. One is the 1980s. In that decade real wages at the tenth percentile declined in most states. This was true of the market incomes of low-end households too, but often to a lesser extent. The second, and more substantial, disjuncture occurs in the 2000s. In roughly twenty of the states, tenth-percentile wages held steady or moved only slightly while tenth-percentile household market incomes fell sharply. As we saw in the previous section, the turn in household incomes was a function largely of big drops in work hours among low-end households.

The period in which low-end wages and low-end market incomes were most closely in sync is the late 1990s. During those years both the tenth-percentile wage level and the tenth-percentile household market income level increased. This period is commonly hailed as the only one among the past several decades in which there was genuine progress in reducing poverty.[18] To be sure, the degree of success was quite limited. As the top chart in Figure 3.1 reveals, the improvement in market incomes at the tenth percentile of the distribution was fairly small. Given the rather dismal record of the 1980s and 2000s, however, these years stand out.

One story sometimes told about the late 1990s is that the key to success in reducing poverty was the 1996 welfare reform. This forced a large number of single women into the labor force, thereby increasing their hours of employment and hence their market incomes. That did indeed happen. But as the lower chart in Figure 3.4 reveals, the resulting increase in employment hours among low-end households was not markedly greater than in the 1980s. What separates the late 1990s from the late 1980s is trends in low-end wages. Due in part to a rise in the federal minimum wage and in part to very tight labor markets, in the late 1990s wages increased throughout the distribution, including at the bottom.[19]

CONCLUSION

Like some other affluent countries, the United States since the 1970s has experienced lengthy periods of economic growth with little or no improvement in the incomes of poor households. Growth can trickle down to the incomes of the poor via three principal routes: an increase in government transfers, an increase in hours of work, and an increase in hourly wages. The analyses in Chapter 2 suggest that a key part of the problem in the United States is that government transfers have failed to rise in concert with economic growth. In this chapter we have examined employment hours and wages.

Both employment hours and wages are implicated in America's trickle down failure. With the exception of the late 1990s, economic growth has not translated into wage growth for Americans at the low end of the labor market. This is widely recognized as a signature feature of the "U.S. model."[20] Defenders of the model have tended to emphasize that its virtue lies on the employment side; weak unions and limited labor market regulations are said to promote job creation, which in principle should result in rising work hours for Americans with limited labor market assets. In fact, employment hours for low-income working-age households did tend to rise fairly sharply during the growth years of the 1980s and 1990s business cycles. But in the 2000s, that ended abruptly. Moreover, in the years during and shortly after the recessions of the early 1980s, early 1990s, and early 2000s, work hours for these households fell precipitously, offsetting the gains achieved during growth years.

From the end of World War II through the middle of the 1970s, the incomes of low-end working-age American households rose steadily.[21] This was due largely to increases in wages and in government benefits. Real wages grew more or less in lockstep with economic growth; and the generosity of key government transfers, particularly to the elderly and to poor single parents, increased regularly. Employment played little role in this progress. The employment rate among working-age adults held steady, and average hours of work declined somewhat.

Since the 1970s the U.S. strategy for poverty reduction has been reversed. Though not always explicitly, many American policy makers have pinned their hopes for poverty reduction on employment. The idea is that even if wages and government benefits are stagnant, economic growth can reduce poverty via jobs. This is not an absurd hope. But thus far it has been largely disappointed. And the deep economic downturn of 2008–9 has surely made things a good bit worse.

What would help? The most common proposed remedies include stronger unions, restraints on globalization, and more education.[22] But the wages of low-end workers and the market incomes of low-end households have been stagnant in many affluent countries.[23] That includes countries with much more powerful labor organizations, ones with varying degrees of exposure to economic internationalization, and nations in which educational attainment has increased more rapidly than in the United States.

In countries where the incomes of low-end households have risen, that has happened largely because policy makers have passed on the fruits of economic growth in the form of more generous government transfers (Chapter 2). This is part of the story in the United States too. In the one period during which low-end household incomes rose, the mid-to-late 1990s, a contributing factor was an increase in the generosity of the Earned Income Tax Credit.[24] Of course, the patterns of the past several decades do not dictate future developments. It is, as many commentators have urged, worth considering ways to increase both the wages and the employment hours of working-age persons at the bottom of the distribution. Yet the experiences of the United States and of other rich nations suggest it is helpful to think about using social policy to boost incomes directly.

4

Generous Social Policy Reduces Material Deprivation

Lane Kenworthy, Jessica Epstein, and Daniel Duerr

Income is an important resource, but it is subject to measurement problems and there are other resources and expenses that affect households' living standards. In recent years, poverty researchers have begun to examine direct indicators of material well-being.

Contemporary interest in indicators of material deprivation was initiated by Peter Townsend in the United Kingdom and by Susan Mayer and Christopher Jencks in the United States.[1] Their studies led to regularized data collection on material hardship in those two countries, via the "Breadline Britain" studies in the United Kingdom[2] and the Census Bureau's Survey of Income and Program Participation (SIPP) in the United States.[3] Other researchers in Europe further advanced the study of material well-being in the 1990s.[4] Material deprivation questions were included in the 1994–2001 European Community Household Panel (ECHP) survey and then in the Survey of Income and Living Conditions (EU-SILC) beginning in the mid-2000s. Interest in indicators of material deprivation has blossomed, with a host of country-specific and comparative studies appearing.[5]

How helpful is economic growth in reducing material deprivation? A few studies have suggested, based on preliminary analysis, that material deprivation tends to be lower in richer countries.[6] This suggests a beneficial effect of growth. But most of the existing research on material hardship has been descriptive, aiming to gauge the extent of deprivation and the degree to which it correlates with income poverty.[7] Explanatory studies have mainly examined individual-level variation, seeking to understand why certain households are materially deprived while others are not.

A MEASURE OF MATERIAL DEPRIVATION

Romina Boarini and Marco Mira d'Ercole have compiled material deprivation data from the EU-SILC for a number of European nations and from country-specific surveys for Australia and the United States (OECD 2008: ch. 7). The data are for the mid-2000s. Each of the surveys asked identical or very similar questions about seven aspects of material deprivation:

- inability to adequately heat home
- constrained food choices
- overcrowding
- poor environmental conditions (e.g., noise, pollution)
- arrears in payment of utility bills
- arrears in mortgage or rent payment
- difficulty in making ends meet.

Boarini and Mira d'Ercole create a summary measure of deprivation by averaging, for each country, the shares reporting deprivation on questions in each of the seven areas.

We use Boarini and Mira d'Ercole's material deprivation measure. It is a deprivation rate—a measure of the average share of the population experiencing various types of material deprivation. One potential concern is that it does not capture the depth of deprivation. But Boarini and Mira d'Ercole also create a measure of the share reporting deprivation in two or more of the seven areas,[8] and it correlates very strongly across countries with the measure we use here.[9]

Like the low-end incomes measure used in Chapter 2, this material deprivation measure is an absolute one.[10] How do these two measures compare? How similar a picture do they offer of the material well-being of the poor? Figure 4.1 shows material deprivation on the vertical axis and low-end incomes on the horizontal axis. The association between the two is negative, as we would expect, and fairly strong. Absolute material deprivation tends to be lower in countries in which absolute incomes at the low end of the distribution are higher.

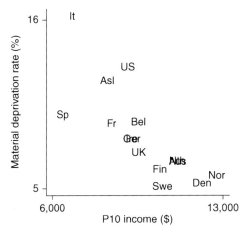

Figure 4.1. Material deprivation and low-end incomes in fifteen countries, 2005

Note: r = -0.77. The axes are truncated (do not begin at zero). For data definitions and sources, see the appendix.

ECONOMIC GROWTH, SOCIAL POLICY, AND DEPRIVATION

In Chapter 2 we discovered that in most countries economic growth has led to rising incomes for low-end households. Has growth been similarly helpful in reducing material deprivation?

The comparative material deprivation data are available at only a single point in time, so we can examine only the cross-sectional relationship between deprivation and per capita GDP. This is shown in Figure 4.2. Surprisingly, there is no association to speak of.

If we had over-time material deprivation data, it seems probable that we would observe a beneficial effect of economic growth. The extent and degree of material deprivation in the United States is much smaller than it was a century or even half a century ago,[11] and that improvement rests heavily on the shoulders of rising per capita GDP. Recent research suggests the same is true of Ireland in the period from the early 1990s through the mid-2000s.[12]

Still, it is puzzling that we observe no association across countries between deprivation and GDP per capita. Why is that? One possibility is measurement error, but we doubt this is the source. The

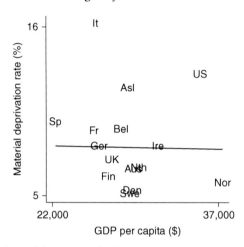

Figure 4.2. Material deprivation by GDP per capita, across countries in 2005

Note: The axes are truncated. Material deprivation is measured in 2005. GDP per capita is measured as an average over 2000–5. The regression line is calculated with Italy omitted. For data definitions and sources, see the appendix.

material deprivation data for thirteen of the fifteen countries come from the same questions in the same survey, the EU-SILC, administered in the same year. The data for the other two countries, Australia and the United States, come from different surveys but similarly-worded questions. Australia does not influence the pattern in Figure 4.2, as its per capita GDP is in the middle of the pack. The United States, on the other hand, does; it has high per capita GDP and high material deprivation. But there is an alternative source of comparative information on material deprivation that suggests reason for confidence in the U.S. score shown in Figure 4.2. The Pew Research Center conducted a survey in the early 2000s that included the following material deprivation questions: "Have there been times during the last year when you did not have enough money (*a*) to buy food your family needed, (*b*) to pay for medical and health care your family needed, (*c*) to buy clothes your family needed?" Among the seven affluent countries included in the Pew survey, measured material hardship was highest in the United States.[13]

The key to the puzzle may instead lie with social policy. Chapter 2 showed that government transfers are the chief mechanism through which economic growth has boosted the incomes of the least well-off. The same may be true for material deprivation. Moreover, deprivation also is likely to be affected by government services. Services enhance people's access to medical care, child care, and housing, and they allow poor households to spend their limited income on other necessities.

The influence of social policy generosity in reducing material hardship can be seen within countries. Brian Nolan and Christopher Whelan report that, across households, the association between (low) income and deprivation tends to be weakest in nations with more generous welfare states and service provision.[14] This is likely a product of the fact that public services alleviate deprivation for households with low incomes.

The cross-country pattern in Figure 4.3 suggests a strong impact of social policy. The material deprivation rate again is on the vertical axis. On the horizontal axis is a measure of social policy generosity: government social expenditures as a share of GDP, adjusted for the fact that some countries spend more because of large elderly populations or high unemployment rates.[15] The measure includes public spending on transfers and services in nine areas: old age, survivors, incapacity-related benefits, health, family, active labor market programs, unemployment, housing, and "other." The association across the countries is negative, as we would expect, and quite strong.

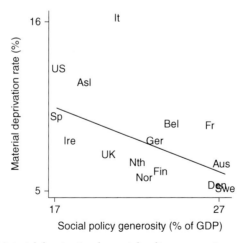

Figure 4.3. Material deprivation by social policy generosity, across countries in 2005

Note: The axes are truncated. Material deprivation is measured in 2005. Social policy generosity is measured as an average over 2000–5. The regression line is calculated with Italy omitted. For data definitions and sources, see the appendix.

Nations with more generous social programs tend to have lower rates of absolute material deprivation.[16]

CONCLUSION

Shifting from incomes to material deprivation buttresses the conclusion reached in Chapter 2. With income as the measure, the comparative evidence suggests that growth has tended to be the principal driver of improved living standards, though government transfers have been the chief conduit through which growth trickles down. With material deprivation as the measure we have less evidence to examine, but what we have suggests an even stronger and more direct impact of social policy.

5

Low Wages Need Not Mean Low Incomes

Two decades ago, Germany was viewed by some comparative observers as history's nearest approximation to the good society. German manufacturing firms thrived in international markets, and their workers enjoyed the world's highest wages. An institutionalized system of pattern bargaining led many middle-size and small firms to follow wage agreements reached in the key manufacturing sectors, which pushed up wages throughout the economy. High wages, coupled with generous government benefits for unemployed and retired workers and their families, meant that Germany had very little poverty.

Today the situation is quite different. Germany's manufacturing firms remain competitive in global markets. But a low-wage sector has emerged in the German economy, and in a relatively short span of time it has grown quite sizeable.[1]

Low-wage employment is likely to persist in Germany. And other European nations may well follow Germany down this path. Is it possible for these countries, and other affluent ones such as the United States, to have a significant low-wage sector without a correspondingly large number of low-income households? Can a country have low wages but also low poverty?

THE RISE OF LOW-WAGE JOBS

As people get richer, they grow more willing to outsource activities such as child care, food preparation, cleaning, and repair work. Little schooling or formal training is needed for some of these tasks, and it is difficult to increase productivity via mechanization or work-process efficiency enhancements. Buoyant demand coupled with low skill requirements and limited productivity improvement create strong pressure for expansion of low-paying service employment.

Economic pressures can be muted by institutions. Strong unions or a steadily rising statutory minimum wage can push up the pay floor, in effect blocking an increase in low-paying service jobs. Strict limits on fixed-term (temporary) or part-time employment can have the same impact. For much of the past several decades this is exactly what has happened in a number of European countries.

But these institutions are changing. Unionization has been on the decline since the 1970s in most rich countries.[2] Figure 5.1 shows union density in 1979 and 2007. The only nations not suffering large declines are the four "Ghent system" countries in which unemployment insurance is tied to union membership—Belgium, Denmark, Finland, and Sweden—plus Norway and Canada.

Despite the fall in union membership, in many countries collective bargaining arrangements have continued to keep the floor of the wage distribution relatively high. That owes to "extension" practices: by agreement between union and employer confederations (most

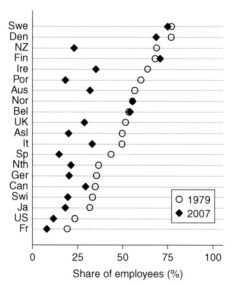

Figure 5.1. Unionization, 1979 and 2007

Note: For data definitions and sources, see the appendix.

nations) or due to government mandate (France), union-management wage settlements carry over to many firms and workers that are not unionized. In a number of countries the share of the workforce whose wages are determined by collective bargaining is much larger than the share of workers who are union members.[3]

With unionization declining, how long will these extension practices hold up? So far Germany is the only country with a moderate or high wage-bargaining coverage rate that has experienced a significant decline in that rate (from 75% in 1990 to about 60% in the mid-2000s). Perhaps Germany will remain an exception, but it seems quite possible that other nations will follow its lead.

If collective bargaining institutions deteriorate, the chief obstacle to falling wages is likely to be a statutory minimum wage. For a long time only a few of the rich countries had a statutory minimum, but more have adopted one in the past decade or so. Simply having a legal minimum is, however, no guarantee of a high wage floor. Some countries, such as France and the United Kingdom, have increased the statutory minimum wage to keep pace with prices or average pay. But others, including the United States and the Netherlands, have allowed significant declines in the inflation-adjusted level of the legal minimum.[4]

Some low-end service jobs are fixed-term positions. An additional obstacle to their expansion is restrictions, via legislation or collective bargaining, on firms' use of temporary employees. These regulations, like unions, have weakened in recent decades. Figure 5.2 shows scores for the level of restrictions on fixed-term employment in 1985 (the earliest available year) and 2007.[5] With the exception of France, the trend in all of the countries with comparatively high levels of restrictiveness has been down.

In some countries, other policy changes have contributed to the rise of low-paying jobs.[6] Germany is one such case. In the 1990s, in an attempt to boost labor force participation via part-time work, the German government created a new employment category: "mini-jobs." These jobs are paid less than 400 euros per month, with the employee exempt from payroll taxes (social security contributions) and income taxes. By the mid-2000s mini-jobs had grown to 15% of total German employment, including 25% in retail trade and 35% in hotels and restaurants.

These changes in economic pressures, institutions, and policies do not guarantee an expansion of low-wage work. A recent study,

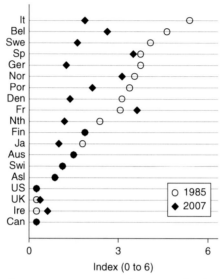

Figure 5.2. Employment protection regulations on fixed-term (temporary) jobs, 1985 and 2007

Note: Higher scores indicate more restrictive regulations. 1985 is the earliest year for which these data are available. There was no change in Australia, Austria, Canada, Finland, Switzerland, and the United States.

Source: OECD, www.oecd.org/employment/protection.

summarized in a volume entitled *Low-Wage Work in the Wealthy World*, examined developments in six countries: Denmark, France, Germany, the Netherlands, the United Kingdom, and the United States.[7] The research teams found significant increases in low-wage employment in the United Kingdom, the United States, and Germany. The institutions resisting such an expansion are comparatively weak in the United States and the United Kingdom, and they have weakened over time in Germany. The Netherlands has moved in the same direction as Germany, though to a much lesser extent. In Denmark and France there has been no rise in low-wage employment. In those two nations the institutions and policies—strong unions in Denmark, a political determination to keep the wage floor high coupled with collective bargaining extension in France—have held firm.

The pattern is clear. Economic pressures for growth of low-wage jobs exist in all rich nations. Whether they produce a rise in low-wage work, and to what degree, is determined by institutions and policy choices.

LOW WAGES, LOW EMPLOYMENT, LOW INCOMES

Citizens and policy makers should worry mainly about low household incomes, not low wages. Earnings and other sources of income are pooled within households. Thus, the fact that a person may have low earnings, even if she works full-time and year-round, does not necessarily give us cause for alarm about her material circumstances.

In recent years, researchers and policy makers have grown increasingly interested in "in-work poverty"—low incomes in households that have one or more employed adults.[8] This concern is merited, but mainly insofar as study of in-work poverty is aimed at enhancing our understanding of low household incomes. It is not helpful to privilege in-work poverty in and of itself. Consider the following hypothetical scenario. A country experiences a rise in employment. In-work poverty—calculated as the number of households with an employed member that are below the poverty line divided by the number of households with an employed member—may increase. That is particularly true if some of the newly employed are low-skilled persons in what previously were workless households. But overall poverty in the country may decrease, because some of the newly employed are second earners who push the incomes of their households above the poverty line. This should be considered an improvement rather than a deterioration in societal well-being. Concern about in-work poverty per se may lead policy makers to miss the big picture.

The question of interest is: Are low wages a significant contributor to low market household incomes?

Recent studies of the rich countries suggest that the principal cause of low market incomes among households with working-age adults is not low wages but rather low employment.[9] A household is more likely to have a low income if it has fewer than two employed adults, and if those employed work only part-time or part of the year, than if it has someone getting paid at a low hourly rate. The magnitude varies across countries, but this holds everywhere. As we saw in Chapter 3, even in the United States, where low wages are thought to be especially problematic, employment hours are a more important determinant of low household incomes than are low-end wage levels (Figure 3.3). To improve household incomes at the low end of the distribution, then, increasing employment is likely to be the better bet.

Still, some households will end up with little more than 35 or 40 hours per week of employment, either because the household has only one adult or because both adults work part-time. If wage levels are low, how will such households escape poverty?

HOW POLICY CAN HELP

The country-level analyses in Chapter 2 (Figure 2.2) suggest that government transfers make a big difference to the incomes of low-earning households.[10] A recent study by the OECD finds this to be true at the household level within countries as well.[11] But if government transfers are too generous, they create work disincentives. Given the importance of employment and work hours for the market incomes of low-end households, policy makers must guard against programs that provide attractive benefits without encouraging or requiring employment. An ideal transfer would be one that both boosts the incomes of low-earning households and promotes employment by able working-age adults.

As it happens, such a program exists. Referred to variously as "in-work benefit" or "employment-conditional earnings subsidy" (I use the latter term here), it is best exemplified by the Working Tax Credit (WTC) in the United Kingdom and the Earned Income Tax Credit (EITC) in the United States. The U.K. credit was introduced in 1971, the American one in 1975.

As of 2010, the EITC provided a tax credit to U.S. households with at least one working adult and a pretax household income up to $45,000. The amount of the credit depends on household size and income. Figure 5.3 shows the benefit levels in 2010 for households with varying numbers of children. The amount of the subsidy increases with earnings up to a certain level, then plateaus, then diminishes with earnings. The credit is refundable; if it amounts to more than the household owes in federal income taxes, the household receives the difference as a cash refund. It therefore functions like a cash benefit. The EITC boosts the incomes of low-earning households, encourages employment, and is relatively inexpensive to administer.[12]

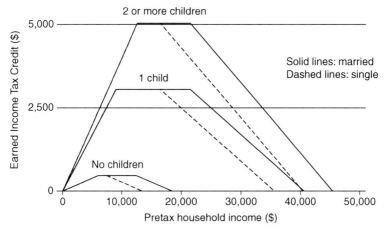

Figure 5.3. U.S. Earned Income Tax Credit (EITC), 2010

Source: Tax Policy Center 2010.

The WTC in the United Kingdom is similar to the EITC in many respects, but it is more generous. It also has a work-time requirement; recipients must work at least 16 hours per week to be eligible for the credit. This prevents people who are paid a healthy hourly rate but work a small number of hours from qualifying.

To be effective, an EITC- or WTC-style employment-conditional earnings subsidy needs to be coupled with a wage floor. Many rich countries now have a statutory minimum wage, and a number of others are likely to adopt one. Where unions remain strong the wage floor can be sustained via collective bargaining.

Without a wage floor, an earnings subsidy may lead to reductions in low-end wage levels, which will offset the improvement in income achieved by the subsidy.[13] This can happen in two ways. First, if the subsidy succeeds in pulling more people into work, the increase in competition for jobs will put downward pressure on wages. Second, regardless of labor supply, employers will be tempted to incorporate the value of the subsidy into the wages they offer.

Additionally, because of the structure of an employment-conditional earnings subsidy, a moderately high wage floor is needed so that the subsidy is feasible.[14] If wages are too low, the amount of the subsidy would have to be especially high in order for it to ensure decent household incomes. The subsidy would then need to extend quite far into the middle class so that the rate at which it is reduced (the slope of the lines on the right side of Figure 5.3) does not become so severe that it creates work disincentives.

Employment-conditional subsidies have spread rapidly over the past decade, becoming a common tool in the social policy arsenal of the world's affluent nations. In a recent review, Herwig Immervoll and Mark Pearson write:

> Arguably, it is possible to discern an evolution in the way that IWB [in-work benefit] schemes are viewed. Even in the mid 1990s, twenty years after such schemes were first introduced in the United Kingdom and the United States, they were being seen as interesting but unusual schemes, worth considering by other countries but certainly not at the heart of discussion about labour market and social policy. By the mid 2000s, it is assumed that such schemes are considered as a matter of course by countries seeking to have a dynamic labour market. Also, whereas in the mid 1990s debates were often at a conceptual level about whether such schemes were a good idea (for example, will such schemes trap economies into using low-wage labour rather than up-skilling the workforce), more recently concerns have become much more practical (for example, the appropriate way of adjusting payments to reflect fluctuations in earnings through a fiscal year). Thus, it seems reasonable to conclude that IWB schemes are now mainstream policies in many countries.[15]

Over the past decade or so, Belgium, Denmark, Finland, France, Germany, the Netherlands, and Sweden are among the countries that have adopted some form of employment-conditional earnings subsidy.[16] In these countries the wage floor is viewed by policy makers as sufficiently high, so boosting low household earnings is not the principal aim. Instead, the goal is to increase employment. Since payroll taxes in these nations tend to be high, the subsidy sometimes consists of a reduction or elimination of taxes paid by employees.

Sweden's Earned Income Tax Credit was introduced in 2007 and increased in subsequent years. Like the U.S. and U.K. credits, it reduces income taxes owed and rises with earnings. Figure 5.4 shows that the Swedish credit is less generous than its American counterpart for low earners (if there is a child) but more generous for middle-income households. On the other hand, if a Swedish household has two earners, each receives the credit separately, so its value is twice as large. And for Americans without children the value of the credit is very small, as Figure 5.3 makes clear.

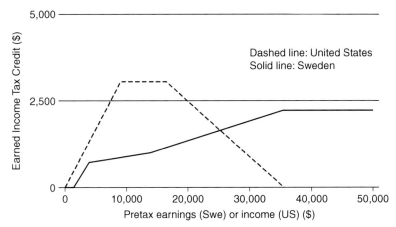

Figure 5.4. U.S. and Swedish Earned Income Tax Credits, 2010

Note: For the United States: single unmarried adult with one child. Sweden: one earner (not contingent on the presence or number of children). PPP conversion: 1 U.S. dollar = 9 Swedish kroner.

Sources: Tax Policy Center 2010; Edmark et al. 2010: Figure 1.

Despite its growing low-wage sector, Germany has not adopted an EITC- or WTC-style earnings subsidy. But that type of subsidy, along with a statutory minimum wage, is likely to be part of Germany's policy debate in coming years. I suspect the same will true of other rich nations whose labor markets follow the German path.

Employment-conditional earnings subsidies are not the only potentially helpful policy. Even if people in low-wage jobs do not end up with low household incomes, their working conditions may leave much to be desired.[17] Policy can help to improve the quality of the work experience.[18] One strategy, suggested by Duncan Gallie, is an auditing procedure, with government setting overall standards for work conditions, letting firms decide how to reach the goals, and then monitoring the outcomes.[19]

In addition, policy makers in a society with a substantial number of low-wage jobs should aim to facilitate exit from such jobs into better ones. Programs to enhance upward mobility out of low-wage jobs include child care and early education, strong primary and secondary schooling, opportunities for lifelong learning, retraining and job placement assistance, and organized job ladders.[20]

OBJECTIONS

Let me address some potential concerns.

"Why should government pick up the tab?" Mandating moderate-to-high wages for low-end service jobs amounts to forcing employers (shareholders, entrepreneurs, heirs, and others) to bear the cost of assuring decent incomes for low-end households. On fairness grounds, that seems preferable to having taxpayers foot the bill.

Compare this, however, to how we think about health insurance, pensions, unemployment insurance, and sickness/disability insurance. Like income, these contribute to economic security and material well-being. In all affluent nations they are financed at least partly by taxpayers, and few object to the fact that firms are not the sole funders. Why, then, is it objectionable for taxpayers to also provide part of the funding for what amounts to insurance compensation for low earnings?

There also is a fairness argument in favor of partial government funding: some small firms cannot afford high wages any more than they can afford to fund their employees' health insurance.

A third consideration in favor of government contribution to the funding of adequate low-end household incomes is the benefit to consumers. If firms bear the full cost, via mandatory moderate-to-high wages, they will pass some of this on to consumers. If taxpayers bear part of the cost, prices for eating out, clothes cleaning, home cleaning, and similar services will tend to be lower. This is akin to provision of public services, which, in a tax system that is roughly proportional, tends to benefit the poor more than the rich (see Chapter 8).

"Low wages are morally objectionable." To some, low wages are objectionable on fairness grounds. In this view it is unjust for firms to pay workers less than a proper wage. This notion has deep roots in the labor movement. It is reflected in demands such as those for "a fair day's pay for a fair day's work" and for a "living wage."

Is it compelling? I don't think so. For most, I suspect, the argument reduces to the previous one—that it is fairer for the burden to be borne by owners than by taxpayers.

For others, though, the argument is about the assessment of value that wages convey. A low wage, in this view, signals that society places a low value on the contribution a person is making to societal well-being. This will tend to have a negative impact on self-esteem. Here too, however, we can refer to pensions, health insurance, and related programs. If employers' contribution to these is modest because taxpayers provide part of the funds, does that too convey a devaluation of an employee's work? If not, what does this tell us about the argument with respect to wages? Is it really the wage that indicates how society perceives a person's contribution, or is it her household's income and material well-being?

"Low wages discourage productivity improvement." High wages encourage employers to raise productivity. Low wages reduce this incentive. In the long run, productivity gains are the source of improvements in living standards. Low wages may therefore be a counterproductive long-term strategy for a country to adopt.

This argument has some appeal, but I am not convinced it is correct. Even in a low-wage country such as the United States, employers regularly seek out ways to increase productivity, whether via changes in the work process or via new technology.[21] They have had limited success for tasks such cleaning offices and hotel rooms, waiting tables, and stocking shelves in supermarkets. But it is not for lack of trying.

"Low wages would undermine the social democratic gestalt." In which countries are the life chances and material well-being of low-end households best? My answer would be the Nordic countries: Denmark, Finland, Norway, and Sweden. I suspect many analysts and policy makers for whom poverty is a key concern would agree. These countries' institutions and policies comprise what is sometimes referred to as the "social democratic model" or the "Nordic model."

Jonas Pontusson offers a helpful delineation of the core features of this model.[22] He identifies six: universalism in the design of social insurance schemes, direct public provision of social services, solidaristic wage bargaining, active labor market policies, policies to promote female employment and gender equality in the labor market, and high levels of investment in public education and policies to equalize educational opportunity.

One view might be that these components are complementary, and that each is needed to ensure that the model produces low inequality and poverty together with economic dynamism. This type of "gestalt" argument, in which the pieces are said to fit together to create a whole that is more than the sum of the parts, is common among comparativists.[23]

Yet national economies often contain features that are not complementary to one another, and in some cases are dysfunctional rather than mutually supportive.[24] Moreover, some recent research suggests that "hybrid" economies, in which institutions and policies are not especially complementary or coherent, sometimes perform quite well.[25] The empirical evidence offers no strong reason to presume that a particular feature is economically functional, much less necessary.

Are high wages at the low end of the labor market ("solidaristic wage bargaining," in Pontusson's formulation) needed for other aspects of the social democratic model to work effectively? Put another way, what would happen in the Nordic countries if low-end wage levels were lower and low-end household incomes were boosted by an employment-conditional earnings subsidy?

One question is whether household incomes would fall. They might not. In an earlier book, *Jobs with Equality*, I compared household incomes for a typical low-end service employee, a hotel room cleaner, in Denmark and the United States as of the mid-2000s.[26] The hourly wage in Denmark at that time was roughly three times that in the United States: $16.36 per hour versus $5.15. But in Denmark, income taxes take a significant chunk. In the United States, income taxes on earnings this low are collected only by state governments, and they are relatively small. Payroll taxes (Social Security and Medicare) also reduce net income for the American household, but again by a fairly small amount. For a household with two children, the Earned Income Tax Credit provides a significant income boost. In the end the Danish and American households turn out to have similar disposable incomes despite the stark difference in wages.

There are important caveats. The high tax payments in Denmark help to fund government services such as health care and childcare/preschool, which enhance living standards for low-income (and other) households. Also, in Denmark, employees get paid vacation equivalent to 15% of their gross earnings, which means the Danish worker receives earnings equivalent to 2,000 hours of work but in fact only has to work 1,740 hours. Still, this comparison suggests that a reduction in wage levels—even a dramatic reduction—need not reduce low-end household incomes.

But what about the social democratic gestalt? Would low wages undermine the functioning of the model as a whole? That is possible. If compensated for via a U.S.- or U.K.-style employment-conditional earnings subsidy, low wages would produce greater targeting in government transfers. By shifting away from universalistic provision, this might weaken the solidarity that underpins the generosity of the existing government programs.[27] A related argument emphasizes the importance of social equality—perceived equality of condition—to the social democratic model.[28] This too might be weakened by the emergence of a low-wage segment of the labor market. A third possibility is that low wages could come to pass in the Nordic countries only if unions were considerably weaker, and in the absence of strong unions these countries would be much less likely to continue their high levels of government services and transfers.

Each of these worries is plausible. Yet history suggests grounds for optimism about the social-democratic model's robustness. In Sweden, the past half century has witnessed a continuous stream of alterations and adaptations: family-friendly programs were introduced and steadily expanded beginning in the 1960s and 1970s; centralized wage bargaining collapsed in the early 1980s; financial markets were deregulated in the 1980s and 1990s, with currency devaluation thereby effectively foreclosed as a government strategy; the 1990s and 2000s have witnessed growing use of private competition in services (schools, child care). Any one of these changes might have been predicted, prior to its occurrence, to trigger the demise of the model. And yet the model persists, arguably as successfully as ever.

Moreover, the social-democratic model varies across the Nordic countries. Large-scale active labor market policy was for the most part confined to Sweden until Denmark began in the 1990s. Even today Finland and Norway make limited use. Finland and Norway also have a very different child care arrangement: a home-care allowance during the first three years. And these four nations differ sharply in the degree of universalism of their transfer programs.

The lesson is that it is difficult to be certain ex ante whether a particular element of an institutional configuration truly is or is not a lynchpin. What seems vital may indeed be so. Or it might not.

"Why is there so much poverty in the United States?" If low wages need not mean low household incomes, why is it that the country with the largest low-wage sector, the United States, has comparatively low incomes at the bottom of its distribution? The question is particularly pointed given that the United States has precisely the type of program that I suggest can help to reduce the connection between low wages and household incomes—an employment-conditional earnings subsidy.

Begin by recalling that most comparative analyses of poverty rates use a relative poverty measure, in which households are deemed poor if their income is below 50% (or 60%) of each country's median. The United States looks bad in these types of analyses in part because its median income is higher than those of most other rich nations. When we use an absolute measure, the United States is closer to the middle of the pack (Chapter 2). Then again, if we turn to a measure of absolute material deprivation, the United States once more is near the bottom of the performance ranking (Chapter 4).

The chief reason the United States has not only low wages but also comparatively low household incomes and material well-being is the stinginess of its government transfers and services. Modest, regularized increases in the Earned Income Tax Credit, unemployment compensation, social assistance (TANF and Food Stamps), housing assistance, public services such as health care and child care, and in the statutory minimum wage would yield significant reductions in income poverty and material deprivation.[29]

CONCLUSION

Low-wage jobs are a prominent feature of the U.S. economy. To the surprise of many observers, the same can now be said of Germany. Changes in economic pressures, institutions, and policies—and also, perhaps, shifts in views about the best way to help immigrants, the young, and the near-elderly into the labor market—make it likely that other countries will follow Germany's lead. But citizens and policy makers should worry far less about low wages for individuals than about low incomes for households. Policy can help to ensure that low wages do not result in low incomes.

6

Targeting May Not Be So Bad

Generous government transfers are a key antipoverty device. But three developments have converged to constrain policy makers: population aging, slower productivity growth, and barriers to higher tax rates imposed by capital mobility.[1] The deep 2008–9 economic downturn has produced severe government budget deficits, which compound the problem.

One possible response is to make greater use of targeting in social policy.[2] Targeted transfers are directed (sometimes disproportionately, sometimes exclusively) to those with low incomes and assets, whereas universal transfers are provided to most or all citizens. Targeted programs are more efficient at achieving redistribution; each dollar or euro or kroner transferred yields a greater reduction in poverty. Increased targeting therefore could be an effective way to maintain or enhance redistribution in the face of diminished resources.

But targeting has a significant potential drawback. Targeted programs tend to have political constituencies that are smaller and less cohesive, engaged, and influential. Such programs thus enjoy less political support.[3] Targeted programs may be more efficient at reducing poverty, but because of their narrower political base the amount transferred via targeted programs may be much smaller than via universal programs. The result, some analysts predict, will be less redistribution.[4]

Walter Korpi and Joakim Palme state the hypothesis in the following way:

> By discriminating in favor of the poor, the targeted model creates a zero-sum conflict of interests between the poor and the better-off workers and the middle classes who must pay for the benefits of the poor

without receiving any benefits.... The debate about the redistributive outcomes of welfare state programs has focused almost exclusively on how to distribute the money available for transfer and has largely ignored variations in the size of the redistributive budget (i.e., the total sum available for redistribution). The degree of redistribution finally achieved depends on the size of the redistributive budget as well as on the degree of low-income targeting.... We can expect a trade-off between the degree of low-income targeting and the size of the redistributive budget, such that the greater the degree of low-income targeting, the smaller the redistributive budget.[5]

Korpi and Palme posit a paradox of redistribution: "the more we target benefits to the poor ... the less likely we are to reduce poverty and inequality."[6]

Is this correct?

TARGETING, UNIVERSALISM, AND REDISTRIBUTION ACROSS COUNTRIES AT COMMON POINTS IN TIME

Do nations that rely more heavily on targeting achieve less redistribution? Korpi and Palme find exactly that.[7] Their measure of targeting-universalism is an index of concentration; it ranges from -1 if the poorest household gets all of the government transfer income (targeted) to 0 if all households get an equal amount of transfer income (universal). Their measure of redistribution is the percentage difference between pretransfer-pretax and posttransfer-posttax income inequality. The data are from the Luxembourg Income Study (LIS).[8] Korpi and Palme examined eleven affluent nations as of the mid-1980s. The pattern among these countries suggested strong support for the hypothesis that greater use of targeting in transfers yields less redistribution.

Figure 6.1 updates the Korpi–Palme analysis. The plots have redistribution on the vertical axis and the targeting-universalism index on the horizontal axis. Included are the ten countries for which data are available for (nearly) the full period from 1980 through the mid-2000s. The LIS data are available in five-year intervals during this period.

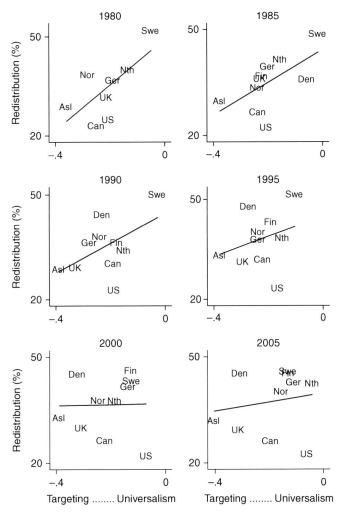

Figure 6.1. Redistribution by targeting-universalism: across countries at common points in time

Note: Redistribution is measured as inequality reduction via transfers, in percentage (rather than absolute) terms. Vertical axes are truncated. For data definitions and sources, see the appendix.

For the first three years—1980, 1985, and 1990—the pattern across the ten nations is consistent with Korpi and Palme's conclusion; countries with greater targeting tend to achieve less redistribution. That is true for 1995 as well, though by that year the pattern begins to get a bit muddled and the slope of the regression line is not as steep.

By 2000 and 2005 the positive association essentially disappears; there is little or no indication of a relationship between targeting and redistribution.

Recall that there are two steps in the hypothesized causal process. First, universalism is thought to increase the size of the redistributive budget. Second, larger redistributive budgets are said to increase redistribution. Universalism's direct impact on redistribution is negative, because benefits go to everyone rather than mainly to the poor. But its indirect effect, via the size of the redistributive budget, is said to be positive and to be much larger in magnitude than its direct negative effect.

What do the data tell us about these two steps in the causal chain? To measure the size of the redistributive budget I use government social expenditures as a share of GDP, adjusted for the unemployment rate and the size of the elderly population (this "social policy generosity" measure is described in the book's appendix).[9] Here's what the data suggest: In each year from 1980 through the mid-1990s, there is a very strong positive association between the size of the redistributive budget and redistribution, exactly as predicted. But the relationship between targeting-universalism and the size of the redistributive budget weakens considerably over time, until by the mid-2000s the positive association has disappeared. The quantity of government social expenditures remains a major determinant of how much redistribution takes place. But the universalism of transfer programs no longer seems to have much impact on the quantity of government social expenditures.

What changed? One key to the story is the shifting position of Denmark. In recent decades, government transfers in Denmark have become more targeted. By the 2000s it had, along with Australia and the United Kingdom, one of the most targeting-heavy transfer profiles among these nations. This runs counter to the stereotype of the highly universalistic Nordic welfare state. And it differs from Finland and Norway; those two countries shift slowly to the right along the horizontal axis in Figure 6.1, in the direction of greater universalism. Sweden barely budges; it begins and ends as one of the most universalistic.

Another surprise is the United States. The United States has long been the poster child for targeting. The standard reference is to its chief social assistance program, known as Aid to Families with Dependent Children (AFDC) up to 1996 and Temporary Assistance for Needy Families (TANF) since then. AFDC/TANF is means-tested and has all of the features commonly associated with "poor relief": a degrading in-person application process, extensive discretion by case-workers, heavy stigma. But AFDC/TANF is a relatively small part of the American welfare state, particularly since the mid-1990s welfare reform.[10] By the early 2000s the share of Americans receiving TANF had dropped to just 2–3 percent. Food Stamps, the other principal means-tested benefit for low-income households, were received by about 7 percent of the population. By that time these two programs were swamped by the Earned Income Tax Credit (EITC), which went to approximately 20 percent of Americans. The EITC is means-tested, but its benefits go only to those with some earnings, so its recipients tend to be a bit higher in the income distribution.

Each of these programs in turn pays out far less than the largest U.S. public transfer program—Social Security. Like public pensions in most countries, Social Security benefits are roughly proportional to earnings, so large transfers end up going to middle-class households. The large (and growing) size of the public pension program relative to other government transfers is the reason America's transfer system ends up scored as heavily universalistic.

This point about the importance of pensions raises a measurement question. Pension payments are a significant portion of government transfers in all rich countries. On one interpretation, counting public pensions in a measure of targeting-universalism or redistribution is misleading, because pension programs are best conceptualized as forced saving. The government requires employed citizens to put money away during their working years and then returns it to them (with interest) in their retirement years. In retirement many people have no income from employment, so the pension they receive appears in the calculations as though it is going to a very poor household. The measures therefore, according to this view, overstate the degree of targeting and the degree of redistribution achieved by transfers.

Peter Whiteford has some calculations of targeting-universalism and redistribution that address this concern.[11] He uses households' position in the income distribution *after* transfers are added and taxes subtracted, rather than before. If a retired couple's income consists solely of a public pension payment, they will be at the very bottom of the distribution according to the calculations in Figure 6.1. In White-ford's calculations they instead might be at the twentieth percentile or even higher, depending on how large their pension check is.[12] An

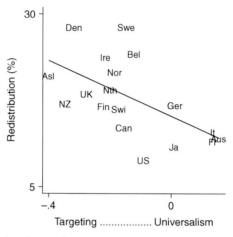

Figure 6.2. Redistribution by targeting-universalism using alternative measures: across countries as of the mid-2000s

Note: Redistribution is measured as inequality reduction via transfers, in percentage (rather than absolute) terms. Unlike in Figures 6.1 and 6.3, redistribution and targeting-universalism are measured here using households' positions in the income distribution after (rather than before) transfers are added and taxes subtracted.

Source: Whiteford 2008: Tables 4.5, 4.6.

additional advantage of Whiteford's calculations is that he is able to include a larger number of countries. A drawback is that the OECD data he uses are less reliable for cross-country comparison than the data from the Luxembourg Income Study.[13]

Figure 6.2 shows that according to Whiteford's calculations, as of the mid-2000s the degree of universalism correlates *negatively* with redistribution; nations that score higher on universalism tend to score lower on redistribution. This by no means settles the question, but it does suggest additional reason to rethink the notion that targeting is an impediment to effective redistribution.

TARGETING, UNIVERSALISM, AND REDISTRIBUTION WITHIN COUNTRIES OVER TIME

What if we look over time within countries? All of the rich countries have faced pressures for reductions in social policy generosity over the past several decades, due to economic globalization and to changes in the balance of power between unions and social democratic parties on one side and employers and right parties on the other. If universalism is good for redistribution, nations with more universal social policy should have fared better in resisting these pressures for cutbacks.

An early skeptical assessment came from Robert Greenstein, who examined the pattern of attempted cuts and successful cuts to targeted programs by the Reagan administration in the United States in the 1980s.[14] Greenstein concluded that these programs fared surprisingly well. Paul Pierson reached a similar conclusion in an analysis of social policy developments under the Reagan administration in the United States and the Thatcher government in the United Kingdom.[15] These are cases in which, according to the conventional view, we might expect to observe significant cutbacks. Recently, Christopher Howard has updated the U.S. story through the mid-2000s. His conclusion echoes those of Greenstein and Pierson:

> Inclusive social programs might have greater moral appeal than targeted programs, based on considerations of equal treatment and social solidarity. Inclusive social programs might have greater technical appeal because of their lower administrative costs. But greater political appeal? Not lately. Evidence from recent decades indicates no significant difference in the political fortunes of upper-tier [universal] versus lower-tier [targeted] social programs. In both tiers, one can find notable examples of political success and political failure. Prescription drug benefits for Medicare were added (1988), repealed (1989), and added again (2003). National health insurance failed (1993–94). Welfare and Food Stamps were periodically retrenched (1981, 1996); Medicaid and the Earned Income Tax Credit were repeatedly expanded (1984–93). Between 1980 and 2000, annual spending grew by 4 percent in the upper tier and 5 percent in the lower tier.[16]

A more systematic comparative analysis of eighteen countries by Kenneth Nelson finds little difference in the trajectories of means-tested benefits (mainly social assistance) and social insurance benefits (old-age pensions, unemployment insurance, and sickness insurance) during the 1990s and early 2000s.[17]

In Figure 6.3 I plot each country's change in redistribution from the mid-1980s to the mid-2000s by its average level of targeting-universalism over this period. (These two dates are at similar points in the business cycle.) The conventional view leads us to expect a

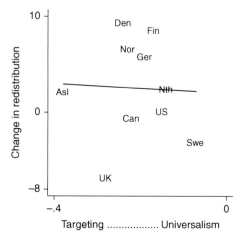

Figure 6.3. Change in redistribution mid-1980s to mid-2000s by level of targeting-universalism

Note: Redistribution is measured as inequality reduction via transfers, in percentage (rather than absolute) terms. Targeting-universalism is measured as the average level from the mid-1980s to the mid-2000s. For data definitions and sources, see the appendix.

positive association; countries with greater targeting (to the left on the horizontal axis) should experience greater declines (or smaller increases) in redistribution over time. That turns out not to hold. Over this two-decade period we see no meaningful association in either direction. The degree to which a country's public transfers are universal does not appear to have had an impact on shifts in its redistributive generosity.

A MORE NUANCED VERSION OF THE HYPOTHESIS

So far I have considered two versions of the universalism-is-better-for-redistribution hypothesis. One suggests that a transfer system more oriented toward universalism than targeting is likely to be larger and to remain so, and it therefore will tend to be more redistributive. The patterns shown in Figure 6.1 suggest this may no longer be true. A second version suggests that within countries, universalistic programs will tend to grow and targeted programs will tend to shrink over time. The studies referenced in the previous section and the pattern shown in Figure 6.3 offer reason for skepticism about that version.

There is, however, a more nuanced version that I have not yet considered. It suggests that what matters is that a nation have universalistic social insurance programs that convey a sense that the country's welfare state mainly serves to provide insurance against risk—old age, sickness, disability, and so on—rather than to redistribute money from rich to poor. In these conditions a country's policy makers will be able, if they wish, to make extensive use of targeting in other programs, because those programs will be seen by the middle class as subsidiary.

This logic might help to explain the over-time developments we observe in Denmark and the United States in Figure 6.1. Denmark's transfer system has shifted from being heavily universalistic in the mid-1980s to comparatively targeting-heavy in the mid-2000s. Yet the size of Danish transfer programs has not declined, and neither, therefore, has its degree of redistribution. In this version of the hypothesis, Denmark was able to do this without a decline in the size of its redistributive budget because it had previously put in place large universalistic programs that succeeded in bringing the middle class on board politically.

The American transfer system has moved in the other direction, from moderately targeted to comparatively universalistic. Yet the size of its redistributive budget has remained relatively low. In this version of the hypothesis, that has happened because, apart from Social Security, the United States never had the kind of large universalistic social insurance programs that would give the American middle class the sense they, rather than the nonworking poor, are key beneficiaries of the welfare state.

This reformulated version of the hypothesis might be correct, but it is difficult to test. The problem is that there are other factors apart from the structure of social programs—union strength, left party influence, government structure, public opinion, and perhaps others—that might account for the fact that Denmark has been able to make greater use of targeting without experiencing a shrinking of its welfare state and that the United States has become more universalistic without a noteworthy increase in the size of its redistributive budget.

CONCLUSION

The hypothesis that targeting in social policy reduces political support and thereby lessens redistributive effort is a sensible one. Yet the experience of the rich countries in recent decades suggests reason to question it. Targeting has drawbacks relative to universalism: more stigma for recipients, lower take-up rates, and possibly less social trust.[18] But targeting is less expensive. As pressures to contain government expenditures mount, policy makers may therefore turn to greater use of targeting. That may not be a bad thing.

7

Public Services Are an Important Antipoverty Tool

Governments in affluent nations provide or subsidize a host of services and public goods. Here is a partial list:

- Physical safety: policing, military
- Assurance of basic liberties: freedom of thought, speech, political participation, religious practice
- Money
- Enforcement of property rights and contracts
- Financial safeguards: limited liability for passive investors, bankruptcy, bank deposit insurance, protection against unauthorized use of credit cards
- Clean air and water
- Street cleaning, removal and disposal of sewage and garbage
- Housing
- Health care
- Disability services
- Elderly services
- Workplace safety
- Consumer safety
- Disaster prevention and relief: firefighting, levies, cleanup, compensation to uninsured victims
- Schooling: early education, K-12, university
- Child care
- Job training

- Job search and placement assistance
- Antidiscrimination enforcement
- Public transportation
- Facilitation of private transportation: roads, bridges, stoplights, enforcement of speed limits, air traffic control
- Public spaces: sidewalks, museums, parks, sports fields, forests, campgrounds, beaches, oceans, lakes, swimming pools, zoos
- Communication, information, and entertainment: support for phone lines, broadband, the Internet, public television and radio programming, subsidization of free private TV and radio networks, libraries, festivals
- Free time: work hours regulations, statutory holidays, mandated vacations, mandated paid parental or family leave.

Social scientists often neglect the contribution of public services to poverty reduction. The reason is simple: it is difficult to measure the degree to which service provision reduces poverty, and what does not get measured tends to be ignored. This is unfortunate. As the findings in Chapter 4 suggest, government services are an important antipoverty tool.

Public services help the poor in two ways. First, they boost living standards directly. Governments subsidize or provide a wide array of services and public goods so that the cost to consumers is small or nil. Second, government services boost the earnings of those at the low end of the income distribution by enhancing human capital, assisting with job search and placement, and facilitating work-family balance.

DIRECT POVERTY REDUCTION VIA SERVICES

When governments provide or subsidize public goods and services, they expand the sphere of consumption for which the cost is zero or minimal. This lifts the living standards of those at the low end of the income distribution, and it frees up their limited income for use in purchasing other goods and services.

How do services redistribute? How is it that they benefit the poor more than the rich? To see this, we need to know who consumes public services and who pays for them.

For any given type of government service, consumption may be progressive, equal, or regressive. That is, the service or public good may be used more by poor households than by affluent ones, about the same by each, or more by the affluent than by the poor. We have no precise measures of the distribution of service consumption, but estimates suggest that it tends to be similar across the income scale or slightly progressive.[1] Let's assume, perhaps conservatively, that the distribution is equal rather than progressive.

Services can be thought of as akin to a cash transfer. If a person receives government-funded health care worth $10,000, it is as though she has been given a $10,000 cash transfer that she then uses to pay for those health services. The same holds for schooling, roads, policing, and virtually every other type of public service. If the rich, the middle class, and the poor each consume roughly the same total dollars or euros or kroner worth of public services, it is equivalent to the government providing a large flat-rate (equal number of dollars or euros) cash transfer to all households.

In a society in which the market distribution of income is unequal, a flat-rate benefit—one that goes in equal amount to all citizens—is redistributive. It boosts the consumption, and hence the living standards, of the poor more than it does for the rich. If my market income is $100,000 and I receive public services worth $20,000, my consumption has increased by 20 percent. If my market income is only $10,000 and I receive government services worth $20,000, my consumption is boosted by 200 percent.

We also need to consider the financing of public services. If the tax system that funds government services is regressive, the provision of services may fail to redistribute. In fact, most rich countries have a tax system that is roughly proportional (see Chapter 8). The effective tax rate is approximately the same for low-income, middle-income, and high-income households; those in each group pay a similar share of their market income in taxes. But because the rich get so much of the market income, they pay a much larger share of the tax *dollars* (or euros or pounds) than the poor.

Services that are financed proportionally and consumed equally are redistributive. Figure 7.1 illustrates this. The tax payment data are estimates for the United States as of the mid-2000s. When all types of

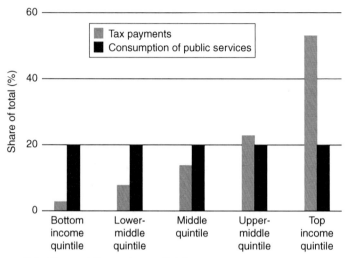

Figure 7.1. How public services redistribute

Note: Estimated distribution of tax payments in the United States in 2004. Hypothetical distribution of consumption of public services. Source for tax payments: author's calculations using data in Chamberlain and Prante (2007).

taxes are taken into account—income, payroll, consumption, and others—the U.S. tax system is proportional; each income quintile pays approximately the same share of its market income in taxes.[2] But because the market distribution of income is quite unequal, the top income quintiles end up paying much more in dollars. The distribution of public service consumption shown in the chart is hypothetical. It is assumed to be equal across the income scale. In this illustration, households in the bottom income quintile pay about 3 percent of the taxes and consume about 20 percent of the government services and public goods.

How large is the redistributive impact of public services? One way to think about this is in relation to government transfers. Estimates by the OECD suggest that services reduce income inequality by only one-quarter to one-half as much as transfers do, depending on the measure used.[3] However, this type of estimate includes only expenditures on health, education, and other public "social" services. It leaves out government spending on physical safety, infrastructure, public spaces, provision of free time (via holidays, paid parental leave, and regulation of work hours), and some of the other public goods and services listed above. If these were included, the estimated redistributive value would be larger.

INDIRECT POVERTY REDUCTION VIA SERVICES

The second way in which public services boost the living standards of the poor is by helping them into employment. Here we tend to think mainly of the K-12 school system, but governments do far more than this. The contribution includes high-quality child care and early (prekindergarten) education, health care, job training, job placement assistance, special services for the mentally and physically disabled, language assistance for immigrants, targeted programs for the young and the elderly, assistance with transportation, and provision of temporary employment when few or no private-sector jobs are available.

All rich countries provide services in each of these areas, but they differ markedly in quantity, distribution, and quality. In terms of expenditures, there is considerable similarity across the affluent nations in the two biggest areas—health care and education. A standard descriptive story contrasts generous European welfare states with the United States. In K-12 education the United States historically was a leader, the first country with truly universal public schooling.[4] As the other rich nations achieved universal K-12 schooling in the second half of the twentieth century, the distribution of American school expenditures turned it from leader to laggard. Decentralized funding with heavy reliance on local property taxes yielded an American public school system in which schools in poorer areas had far less money to spend on teachers, equipment, and infrastructure.[5] Things have improved in the past several decades as state governments have provided a growing share of public school funds,[6] but large inequalities across states continue to disadvantage children in poorer parts of the country. In health care, the United States provides access to health-care services via Medicaid, Medicare, and the State Children's Health Insurance Program (S-CHIP). And overall the U.S. government spends as much on health care, relative to GDP, as most other rich nations. But a significant portion of American health-care expenditure goes to administrative costs and to advanced technology that is of limited benefit to the poor. And stinginess in access to Medicaid by some state governments coupled with refusal by some health-care providers to accept Medicaid patients mean true access is very uneven.[7]

The largest differences across countries are in services other than health care and education.[8] The Nordic countries in particular stand apart from other rich nations.[9] Since the mid-1960s, Sweden, Denmark, and Norway, and later Finland, have put in place and steadily expanded an array of services that enhance the capabilities of people who grow up in relatively poor households and help them balance employment with family commitments throughout the life course. At the center of this is paid parental leave, child care, and early education. Parents typically are able to take a paid leave during a child's first year. They can then put the child in high-quality low-cost public child care and preschool centers after the first year and up to kindergarten. This facilitates employment for parents, especially mothers, and it boosts the cognitive and noncognitive skills of children from disadvantaged homes. After finishing formal schooling, young, middle-aged, and older adults can take advantage of various supports collectively referred to as "active labor market programs"—

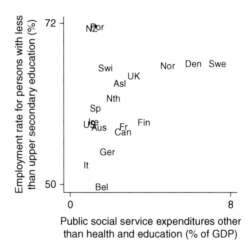

Figure 7.2. Employment rate among persons with less than upper secondary education by public social service expenditures other than health and education, mid-2000s

Note: Employment rate is for 2007; employed persons as a share of persons age 25–64. Public social service expenditures are for 2003.

Sources: OECD 2009: Table D; Castles 2008: Table 1.

from specialized training to job placement to assistance with geographical relocation, among others.

Figure 7.2 offers one piece of evidence that suggests these types of policies may help. On the vertical axis is the employment rate among 25-to-64-year-olds with less than upper secondary schooling. On the horizontal axis is the share of GDP spent on public social services other than health care and education. Denmark, Norway, and Sweden are the biggest spenders, and apart from New Zealand and Portugal their employment rates among the less-educated are the highest. Given that the Nordic countries have generous social assistance benefits and other supports that make it possible to live reasonably well without employment, this performance is impressive.

CONCLUSION

The analyses in Chapter 4 suggest that countries with larger public social expenditures tend to have less material deprivation. Public services are a key part of the story, but an often-overlooked one. Services improve the capabilities and employment prospects of people from disadvantaged homes and neighborhoods, and they directly boost living standards by expanding the sphere of consumption for which the cost is small or nil.

8

The Tax Mix Matters Less Than
We Thought

To provide transfers and services, governments must tax. In affluent countries the principal sources of government revenue are taxes on income (individual and corporate), payroll, and consumption. What is the optimal mix among these three types of taxes?

From the point of view of effective social policy, there are three chief desiderata: progressivity of the tax system, the quantity of tax revenues generated, and compatibility with economic growth and employment growth. How do the three types of taxes contribute to the achievement of these goals? Current wisdom suggests the following:

- Income taxes tend to be progressive, whereas taxes on payroll and consumption usually are regressive.
- Payroll and consumption taxes are more useful than income taxes for increasing revenues.
- Taxes on income and payroll are the least conducive to economic growth. Payroll taxes impede growth of employment.

What should governments do? I begin with some descriptive information on cross-country differences and over-time trends in the tax mix in affluent nations. I then examine the empirical evidence on tax progressivity, the quantity of revenues raised via taxation, and the effects of taxes on economic growth and employment growth. The comparative experience of the past few decades yields some surprises.

THE TAX MIX ACROSS COUNTRIES
AND OVER TIME

Figure 8.1 shows tax revenues as a share of GDP in 2007, the peak year of the most recent complete business cycle, in twenty rich nations. It also shows revenues as a share of GDP for taxes on income and for taxes on consumption plus payroll. There is considerable variation across the countries both in total tax revenues and in the tax mix. Taxes total just over a quarter of GDP in the United States and Japan compared to half of GDP in. Denmark and Sweden. In most countries, revenues from consumption and payroll taxes are greater than those from income taxes, but in Denmark, New Zealand, Canada, Australia, and the United States the reverse is true.

Figure 8.2 shows trends over time in the average levels (not weighted by country size) for the twenty nations. The average for total tax revenues rose from 25 percent of GDP in 1960 to 38 percent in 2007. Virtually all of that increase occurred by the late 1980s, when the average reached 37 percent. Since then the mean level has been

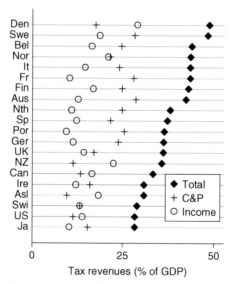

Figure 8.1. Total tax revenues and the tax mix, twenty countries, 2007
Note: C&P = consumption and payroll. For data definitions and sources, see the appendix.

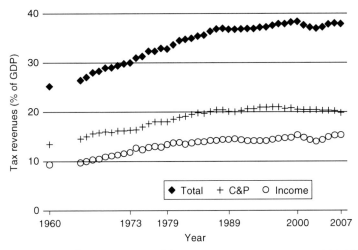

Figure 8.2. Total tax revenues and the tax mix, twenty countries, 1960–2007
Note: C&P = consumption and payroll. For data definitions and sources, see the appendix.

essentially flat. A similar pattern holds for income taxes and for consumption plus payroll taxes.

PROGRESSIVITY

Taxes can redistribute. If those with high incomes pay a larger share of their income in taxes than do those with low incomes, the tax system is "progressive"—that is, redistributive. If the rich and poor pay a similar share of their incomes, the tax system is termed "proportional"; it does not alter the pretax distribution of income. If the poor pay a larger share than the rich, the tax system is "regressive."

Income taxes almost always are progressive; those with higher incomes pay at higher rates. Deductions and exemptions often reduce the degree of progressivity, but they do not eliminate it. Consumption taxes and payroll taxes usually are regressive.[1] Typically they are levied at a flat rate, which in principle should make them proportional. But the poor (by necessity) tend to spend a larger share of their income than the rich, which means a larger share of their income is subject to consumption taxes. And payroll taxes often are capped;

earnings above the cap are not subject to the tax. This means a larger portion of the earnings of low and middle earners is subject to payroll taxes.

Given these considerations, from a redistributive point of view it seems logical to prefer income taxation over taxes on consumption and/or payroll. In practice, though, taxation tends to affect the degree of redistribution to only a limited extent regardless of the tax mix. In the world's affluent nations, redistribution is achieved mainly via government transfers and provision of services, rather than via taxation.[2]

Figure 8.3 compares the differing redistributive impact of taxes with that of transfers in nations for which such a calculation is possible using Luxembourg Income Study data.[3] Inequality reduction via taxes is measured as the Gini coefficient for pretransfer-pretax household income minus the Gini for pretransfer-posttax income. Inequality reduction via transfers is measured as the Gini coefficient for pretransfer-pretax income minus the Gini for posttransfer-pretax income. In many countries the tax system achieves little or no reduction of income inequality. And in fact, the picture shown here overstates the degree of inequality reduction by taxes, because consumption taxes, which are regressive, are not included.[4] By contrast,

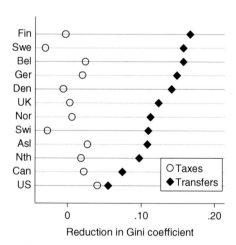

Figure 8.3. Inequality reduction via taxes and government transfers, 2000

Note: Taxes include income and payroll, but not consumption. For data definitions and sources, see the appendix.

transfers do redistribute. In some countries they reduce income inequality quite substantially.

The principal contribution of taxes to redistribution is indirect: taxes provide the revenues that fund government transfers and services. Figure 8.4 makes this clear. In the top chart, the amount of inequality reduction achieved via government transfers is on the vertical axis and total tax revenues as a share of GDP is on the horizontal. The association is positive and quite strong ($r = +0.74$). The lower chart switches the vertical axis from redistribution via transfers to redistribution achieved via public services. Here too we observe a positive association. It is not as strong ($+0.41$). This is in part because expenditures on some important types of government services and public goods are not well-measured (see Chapter 7). It also is partly because the most expensive services provided by governments are health and education, and the rich countries spend similar amounts on these; if expenditures on health and education are removed, the positive association between tax revenues and inequality reduction via services is stronger ($+0.60$).

What matters most from the point of view of redistribution, then, is the quantity of tax revenues rather than the progressivity of the tax mix. The choice between income taxes versus consumption and payroll taxes is not irrelevant to progressivity, but the progressivity of the tax system matters far less than how much revenue is raised.

A comparison of two high-tax countries with sharply differing tax mixes sheds further light. Denmark and Sweden have the largest tax takes among the rich countries; in 2007, at the peak of the 2000s business cycle, taxes accounted for half of GDP in both countries (Figure 8.1). But these revenues were generated in very different ways. In Denmark, taxes on personal and corporate income collect 29 percent of GDP, consumption taxes 16 percent, and payroll taxes just 1 percent. In Sweden, income taxes collect roughly 20 percent of GDP, consumption taxes 13 percent, and payroll taxes 15 percent.

Denmark's tax system relies much more heavily on income taxes than Sweden's. Indeed, Denmark draws far more revenue from income taxes than any other rich country. Yet in Figure 8.3 we see that Sweden's tax system is only slightly more regressive than Denmark's (that is true in other years as well). And since consumption taxes cannot be included in those calculations and Denmark is a bit heavier

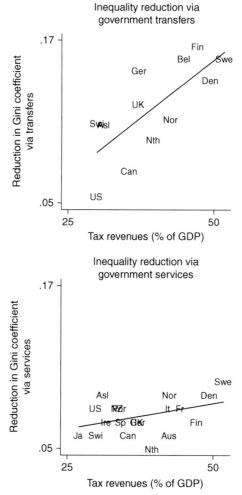

Figure 8.4. Inequality reduction via government transfers and government services by tax revenues, 2000

Note: The range of values on the vertical axis is the same in both charts. For data definitions and sources, see the appendix.

than Sweden in consumption tax use, it is possible that the two countries are virtually identical in their degree of tax progressivity. Moreover, even if the Danish tax system is slightly less regressive than Sweden's, the difference is swamped by the amount of redistribution achieved via transfers and services in both countries.

THE QUANTITY OF TAX REVENUES

What tax mix is most conducive to generation of a large quantity of revenues? The dominant view is that consumption and payroll taxes are more effective revenue sources than taxes on income.[5] There are three reasons why.

First, taxes on consumption and payroll may be less visible to citizens and therefore generate less political opposition. Income tax payments are highly visible. For those with middle or high incomes, they tend to be large. And even though they typically are deducted from one's paycheck on a regular basis, once a year at tax time we see the cumulative total. This leads taxpayers to perceive income tax payments as a large lump sum quantity.

Consumption taxes too may be large. But they are paid in small increments, and there is no point during the course of the year when the taxpayer is made aware of the total amount paid. The same is true of payroll taxes (including social security contributions). They too may be quite large, and the taxpayer can easily check her or his end-of-the-year pay stub to see the grand total deducted over the course of the year. But many do not, so like consumption taxes they are likely to be perceived as smaller than the income tax.

Second, consumption and payroll taxes are considered by many economists to be more efficient than income taxes, because they vary less by income. More efficient taxes might induce less opposition from citizens and interest groups to increases in taxation.[6]

Third, income taxes are viewed as more vulnerable than consumption and payroll taxes to cross-national competition. That is particularly true for corporate income taxes, since firms are more mobile than people. But individuals too are thought to be more likely to decamp in search of a lower income tax rate than a lower tax rate on consumption or payroll.

A dissenting voice is Steffen Ganghof, who notes that Denmark has very high tax revenues (as a share of GDP) and yet relies heavily on income taxation.[7] Ganghof suggests that pressure for low income tax rates applies mainly to a particular type of income: corporate profits and capital income. There is much less pressure on taxation of wage and salary income. Hence, if policy makers are willing to tax wage and salary income at a different rate than capital income and corporate profits (a so-called "dual income tax"), as Denmark does, they can choose to rely mainly on income taxes rather than consumption and payroll taxes to finance a large welfare state.

The standard view suggests both a cross-sectional pattern and an over-time one. Countries that collect a larger share of GDP in taxes should rely more heavily on consumption and payroll taxes to do so; that is, we should observe a positive cross-country association between total tax revenues as a share of GDP and consumption and payroll tax revenues as a share of total tax revenues. And countries that have increased tax revenues as a share of GDP over the past several decades should have done so mainly by increasing consumption and/or payroll tax revenues; we should observe a positive over-time association within nations.

Figure 8.5 shows the cross-country pattern in 1960 and in 2007. If Denmark is excluded as a special case, the correlation jumps from +0.20 in 1960 to +0.50 in 2007. At first glance, this change in the cross-country pattern appears to support the hypothesis that consumption and payroll are the key to revenue increases. It seems to imply that countries in which tax revenues increased are ones in which the consumption and payroll tax share rose; in other words, they generated more tax revenues via increased consumption and/or payroll taxes.

It turns out, however, that this is not what occurred. If it had, the nations with rising tax revenues would have moved not only higher

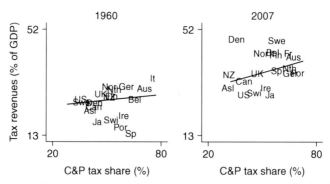

Figure 8.5. Total tax revenues by the consumption and payroll tax share: across countries, 1960 and 2007

Note: C&P tax share = consumption tax revenues plus payroll tax revenues as a share of total tax revenues. Regression lines are calculated with Denmark omitted; see the text for discussion. For data definitions and sources, see the appendix.

on the vertical axis in the second chart in Figure 8.5 but also to the right on the horizontal axis. Yet that is not what we observe. Instead, countries that began to the right on the horizontal axis in 1960 moved higher on the vertical axis but not farther to the right. This means these countries were increasing tax revenues, but not disproportionately via consumption and/or payroll taxes.

Figure 8.6 allows us to better explore the over-time patterns within countries. The charts plot total tax revenues by the consumption and payroll share of total tax revenues for each country. I include six years: 1960, 1973, 1979, 1989, 2000, and 2007. Aside from 1960, which is the earliest year for which the data are available, these are business-cycle peak years, which makes them useful for comparison. What we observe is inconsistent with the conventional view. Tax revenues grew in most countries. But in only two of the twenty nations, Sweden and the Netherlands, do we observe the hypothesized positive over-time association. In a number of countries— Austria, Canada, Finland, Germany, Ireland, New Zealand, Norway, Portugal, Switzerland, the United Kingdom—total tax revenues rose but with no change in the share from consumption and payroll taxes. In others—Australia, Belgium, Denmark, France, Italy, Spain—a rise in tax revenues occurred despite a reduction, rather than an increase, in the consumption and payroll tax share.[8]

Countries with expanding tax revenues have not accomplished this primarily via increased revenues from consumption and/or payroll taxes. Nations that had a larger consumption and payroll tax share as of 1960 tended to raise their tax take more in the ensuing several decades. But apart from Sweden and the Netherlands, they did so as much via heightened income taxes as via increased consumption and/or payroll taxes.[9]

COMPATIBILITY WITH ECONOMIC
GROWTH AND EMPLOYMENT GROWTH

A key worry about generous social policies is that they may reduce economic growth. Yet comparative research suggests little if any negative impact of social policy on growth performance.[10]

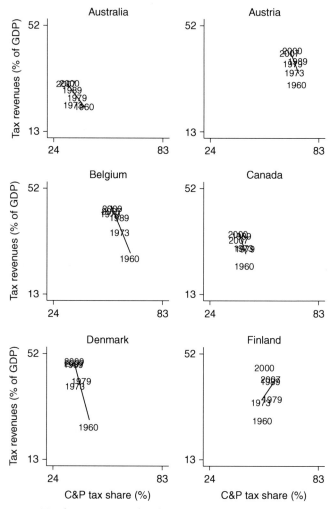

Figure 8.6. Total tax revenues by the consumption and payroll tax share: over time within countries

Note: See the note to Figure 8.5. For data definitions and sources, see the appendix.

What about the taxes that fund government transfers and services? Figure 8.7 shows economic growth rates from 1979 to 2007 by tax revenues as a share of GDP averaged over those years. Nations that began this period with lower per capita GDP tended to grow more rapidly simply by virtue of starting behind; I adjust the growth rates

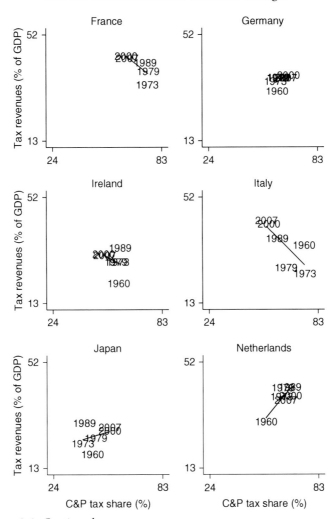

Figure 8.6. Continued

for this "catchup" effect. There is no noticeable association between the quantity of tax revenues and the (catchup-adjusted) rate of economic growth across these twenty countries. Of course, this simple picture does not fully answer the question. But more detailed studies tend to reach a similar conclusion.[11]

Why is that? In an influential contribution, Peter Lindert suggests that it is a function of the tax mix.[12] Lindert points out that the

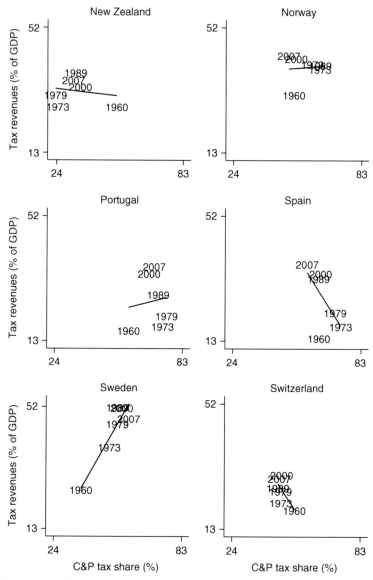

Figure 8.6. Continued

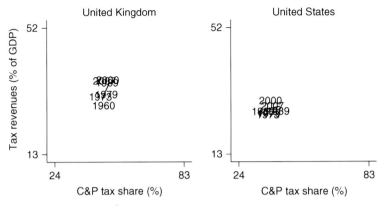

Figure 8.6. Continued

nations with the most generous social policies, the Nordic ones, rely disproportionately on consumption taxes. These, he says, create far less in the way of investment and work disincentives than do taxes on individual and corporate income.

Are consumption taxes more conducive to economic growth than income (individual and corporate) and payroll taxes? The com-

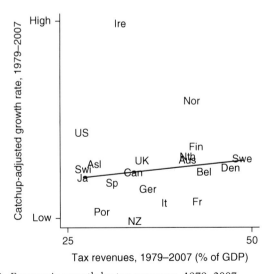

Figure 8.7. Economic growth by tax revenues, 1979–2007

Note: Economic growth is adjusted for catchup; see the text for discussion. The regression line is calculated with Ireland omitted. For data definitions and sources, see the appendix.

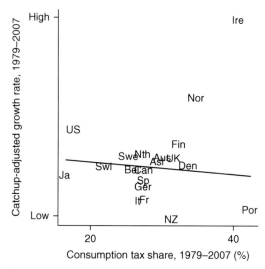

Figure 8.8. Economic growth by the consumption tax share, 1979–2007

Note: Economic growth is adjusted for catchup; see the text for discussion. The regression line is calculated with Ireland omitted. For data definitions and sources, see the appendix.

parative experience of the past three decades offers little support. Figure 8.8 plots catchup-adjusted economic growth rates by the share of tax revenues that come from consumption taxes. Ireland appears to fit the hypothesis nicely, but Ireland's growth experience during these three decades was exceptional in so many respects that attributing it to the country's tax mix seems dubious. If Ireland is discounted we see no association. The same is true if the quantity of total tax revenues is controlled for.

Above a certain level, taxes on income surely do impede economic growth. They will reduce investment or work effort, lead to capital and/or labor flight, or generate a problematic level of popular opposition. But it may well be that none of the existing rich countries exceeds that level. Consumption taxation is a complement, not a substitute; it allows policy makers to generate revenues well beyond what would be growth-compatible via income and payroll taxes alone.

What about employment? Here research has tended to suggest reason for worry about heavy use of payroll taxes. The concern has to do mainly with the way in which these taxes raise the price of labor in low-productivity services. Fritz Scharpf put the point as follows:

The negative impact on service employment is particularly acute in those countries which, like Germany and France, rely to a large extent on payroll taxes for the financing of the welfare state. In Germany, for instance, 74% of total social expenditures were financed through workers' and employers' contributions to social insurance systems in 1991, and in France that was true of 82%. In Germany, these contributions presently amount to about 42% of the total wage paid by the employer.... If the net wage of the worker cannot fall below a guaranteed minimum [the level of unemployment benefits and social assistance], the consequence is that any social insurance contributions, payroll taxes, and wage taxes that are levied on jobs at the lower end of the pay scale cannot be absorbed by the employee but must be added to the total labor cost borne by the employer .... As a consequence, a wide range of perfectly decent jobs, which in the absence of payroll taxes would be commercially viable, are eliminated from the private labor market.[13]

Several studies have found supportive evidence: employment, particularly in low-end services but also overall, has tended to grow more slowly in nations with heavier taxes on payroll.[14]

Figure 8.9 plots change in the employment rate between the peak business cycle years of 1979 and 2007 by the payroll tax share during

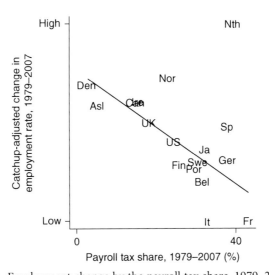

Figure 8.9. Employment change by the payroll tax share, 1979–2007

Note: Employment change is adjusted for catchup; see the text for discussion. The regression line is calculated with the Netherlands omitted. Austria, New Zealand, and Switzerland are missing due to lack of 1979 employment-rate data. For data definitions and sources, see the appendix.

this period. As with economic growth, I adjust employment change for the countries' starting (1979) employment rates, as those beginning lower should have had an easier time generating an increase. The pattern suggests a fairly strong negative association. There are a number of other policies and institutions that may influence employment growth and with which a high payroll tax share is correlated across these countries, but controlling for them does not make the association go away.[15]

On the other hand, controlling for those other institutions and policies does reduce the estimated magnitude of the effect. And there also is the matter of the Netherlands, which relies heavily on payroll taxes but nevertheless has enjoyed successful employment performance since the 1970s. Looking at changes in the employment rate overstates the degree of Dutch success somewhat, as much of its employment rise took the form of short-hour part-time jobs.[16] Still, it was genuine success.

Is there a rationale for heavy payroll taxes? In the countries in which payroll taxes are most significant—France, Germany, the Netherlands, and Spain—the welfare state is "Bismarkian."[17] Pensions, unemployment benefits, and sickness benefits are administered jointly by unions, employers, and the state. These programs are financed by payroll taxes, paid by both employers and employees. In these systems, payroll tax payments are referred to as "social security contributions" rather than taxes. Though the programs operate on a pay-as-you-go basis—money paid in goes directly to current beneficiaries—they are popularly viewed as akin to private insurance. People tend to think of their contributions as investments set aside to benefit them directly in the event of job loss, illness, disability, or retirement. This is an illusion, but it is an illusion that has, arguably, underpinned the generosity of these programs. Were the programs to be financed largely by income and/or consumption taxes, they might end up less generous because public support would be narrower and shallower.

Nevertheless, there now is relatively widespread sentiment that the employment cost of such heavy reliance on payroll taxes outweighs this advantage. And several of these countries have moved, if somewhat tentatively, to alter this financing structure and/or its impact on employment.[18] In 1990, France introduced a new tax on personal income (the CSG) in order to reduce reliance on payroll taxes. This was only a partial step, though, with payroll taxes still accounting for four-fifths of the revenues that support French social policy.[19] Shifting taxation from payroll to general income taxes was a key item of discussion in Germany's "Alliance for Jobs" in the late 1990s. But agreement to reform the tax system was not reached, and as a result, in the early 2000s, Gerhard Schroeder's social democratic government imposed cuts in unemployment benefit levels and duration.[20] More recently, Germany reduced the social security contribution rate slightly, and compensated with an increase in its consumption (value-added) tax rate. Low-paying jobs in Germany ("mini-jobs") are exempt from social security contributions. The Netherlands and France also have introduced partial or full exemptions on social contributions for certain types of low-end jobs.

Why have the shifts been relatively limited? This is a classic "insider–outsider" dilemma.[21] Heavy payroll taxes impose costs on the nonemployed. Yet because they underwrite generous social insurance programs, they are happily paid and strongly supported by those with steady jobs and their families. It is in the (short-term) interest of these "insiders" to maintain the status quo.

CONCLUSION

Does the tax mix matter for effective social policy? If so, how much and in what ways? Current thinking holds that it matters a great deal. Income taxes are viewed as better for progressivity. Consumption and payroll taxes are seen as more conducive to revenue generation. Taxes on consumption are believed to be less of an impediment to economic growth than taxes on income and payroll. Income and consumption taxes are thought to be better for employment growth than payroll taxes.

The comparative empirical record offers little or no support for three of these four propositions. Instead, it suggests the following:

- Income taxes are indeed the most progressive of the three major types of taxes. But taxation tends to have relatively little direct impact on the income distribution. Transfers and services are far more important.

- Consumption and payroll taxes have not been the key to expansion of tax revenues in recent decades. The nations that have increased revenues (as a share of GDP) have done so as much via income taxes.

- Countries relying more heavily on income taxes have not suffered slower economic growth.

- Nations that rely more heavily on payroll taxes do appear to have had slower employment growth over the past few decades, though the Netherlands is a significant exception.

What do these findings imply for policy makers seeking an optimal tax mix? Perhaps most important, they suggest that countries have a good bit of leeway to choose.[22] Apart from the adverse employment consequences of very high payroll taxes, the tax mix appears to neither impose large costs nor generate substantial benefits.

For countries that currently raise enough tax revenues to fund generous transfers and services, adjusting the tax mix therefore probably need not be a priority. The one exception is nations in which payroll taxes are especially heavy.

For a country seeking to increase tax revenues, the chief constraint may be its current mix. From a political perspective, diversity of tax types is helpful. The affluent nation with the least diverse mix is Denmark, which relies heavily on income taxes, moderately on consumption taxes, and very little on payroll taxes. In some respects that is a desirable mix. But it would be difficult for other countries to get to a Danish-style tax mix now, as for most that would require a sizeable increase in income taxation. Instead, countries that deem it desirable to increase tax revenues are likely to find it most politically feasible to generate new revenues from taxes that currently are low. In the United States, for instance, if the political will existed to increase taxation by around 5 or 10 percent of GDP, the easiest way to do that might be via a national consumption tax, as consumption taxes currently account for a relatively small share of American taxation.

9

The Aim Is Not Spending Per Se

A commonplace view holds that a market-liberal political economy is best for the rich while a social-democratic one is best for the poor. Some recent research suggests reason to question this. Analyses by Willem Adema of the OECD, by Adema and Maxime Ladaique, and by Price Fishback conclude that the quantity of social expenditures in the United States is similar to or greater than in Denmark and Sweden, two nations long considered large-welfare-state exemplars.[1]

How so? Government social transfers account for a much larger share of GDP in Sweden and Denmark. But the U.S. government distributes more benefits in the form of tax breaks rather than transfers than do the two Nordic countries; Denmark and Sweden tax back a larger portion of public transfers than the United States does; private social expenditures, such as those on employment-based health insurance and pensions, are greater in the United States; and America's per capita GDP is larger.

Is social spending in the United States really similar to that of the world's most generous welfare states? If so, are America's poor better off than we thought?

A MORE COMPLETE MEASURE OF SOCIAL EXPENDITURES

The standard indicator of social policy effort is gross public social expenditures as a percentage of GDP. The first row in Table 9.1 shows that, unsurprisingly, Denmark and Sweden are much higher than the United States on this measure.

Table 9.1. Social expenditures and bottom-income-decile living standards in Denmark, Sweden, and the United States, mid-2000s

	Denmark	Sweden	United States
Gross public social expenditures as a share of GDP, mid-2000s (%)	27	29	16
Net public and private social expenditures per person, mid-2000s (2000 U.S. dollars)	$7,400	$9,100	$10,000
Average posttransfer-posttax income of households in the bottom income decile, mid-2000s (2000 U.S. dollars per equivalent person)	$9,600	$8,200	$5,900
Average net government transfers received by households in the bottom income decile, mid-2000s (2000 U.S. dollars per equivalent person)	$6,800	$5,300	$2,900
Average share of the population reporting deprivation in seven areas, mid-2000s (%)	5	5	13

Note: Row 1 source: OECD 2010; Row 2 source: Author's calculations using data in Adema and Ladaique 2009: Table 5.5; Rows 3 and 4 source: Author's calculations using Luxembourg Income Study data; Row 5 source: OECD 2008: 186–8.

Now shift to net (rather than gross) public and private (rather than public alone) expenditures per person (rather than as a percentage of GDP, with purchasing power parities used to convert Danish and Swedish kroner into year-2000 U.S. dollars). According to the calculations by Adema and Ladaique, we get a very different picture.[2] By this measure the United States is the biggest spender. These numbers are in the second row in Table 9.1.

ARE AMERICA'S POOR BETTER OFF THAN WE THOUGHT?

This looks like good news for the poor in the United States. Is it? Unfortunately, no. These adjustments change the story with respect to the aggregate quantity of resources that goes to social protection in the three countries, but they have limited bearing on poverty reduction and on the living standards of the poor.

Begin with tax breaks. Researchers count as "social" those designed to provide support in circumstances that adversely affect people's well-being. In the United States these disproportionately go to the affluent and the middle class. The chief ones are tax advantages for employer contributions to private pensions and to private health insurance. These do little to help people at the low end of the distribution, who often work for employers that do not provide retirement or health benefits. One important tax benefit for low-income households is the Earned Income Tax Credit (EITC), but it is already included in the standard OECD data on government social expenditures. Another is the child tax credit, but it is only partially refundable and so of limited value to low-income households, many of whom do not owe any federal income tax.

Next consider tax "clawbacks" in the Nordic countries. Public transfer programs in Denmark and Sweden tend to be "universal" in design: a large share of the population is eligible for the benefit. This is thought to boost public support for such programs. But it renders them very expensive. To make them more affordable, the government claws back some of the benefit by taxing it as though it were regular income. All countries do this, including the United States, but the Nordic countries do it more extensively. Does that hurt their poor? Very little. The tax rates tend to increase with household income, so much of the tax clawback hits middle- and upper-income households.

What is the impact of private social spending? In the United States this accounts for roughly two-fifths of all social expenditures. It consists mainly of employer contributions to health insurance and employment-based pension benefits. Here too the picture changes a great deal on average, but not much for the poor. Employer-based health insurance and pension plans reach few low-income households.

So how well-off are the poor in the United States, with its "hidden welfare state",[3] compared to social-democratic Denmark and Sweden? If you have read Chapters 2 and 4, you know the answer. If not, here is a brief summary.

One measure is average posttransfer-posttax income among households in the bottom decile of the income distribution. The third row in Table 9.1 shows my calculations using the best available comparative data, from the Luxembourg Income Study (LIS).[4] (The numbers are adjusted for household size. They refer to a household with a single adult. For a family of four, multiply by two.) There is a pretty sizeable difference, not in America's favor.[5]

What is the source of this cross-country difference in the incomes of low-end households? It is entirely a function of government transfers. Again using the LIS data, I have calculated mid-2000s averages for households in the bottom income decile for the three chief sources of household income: earnings, net government transfers (transfers received minus taxes paid), and "other" income (money from family or friends, alimony, etc.). Average earnings are virtually identical across the three countries, at about $2,500. The same is true for "other" income, which averages around $500 in each of the three. Where bottom-decile Danish and Swedish households fare much better than their American counterparts is in net government transfers, as shown in the fourth row of Table 9.1.[6]

Price Fishback points to one other key difference between these countries: "Public services not counted in disposable income, like health care and education, likely are better for the very poor in the Nordic countries than in the United States."[7] It is difficult to measure the impact of services on living standards with any precision. One indirect way to assess their effect is to switch from income to material deprivation. As described in Chapter 4, two OECD researchers, Romina Boarini and Marco Mira d'Ercole, have compiled material deprivation data from surveys in various rich nations as of the mid-2000s.[8] Each of the surveys asked identical or very similar questions about seven indicators of material hardship: inability to adequately heat one's home, constrained food choices, overcrowding, poor environmental conditions (e.g., noise, pollution), arrears in payment of utility bills, arrears in mortgage or rent payment, and difficulty in making ends meet. Boarini and Mira d'Ercole create a summary measure of deprivation by averaging, for each country, the shares of the population reporting deprivation on questions in each of these seven areas. The shares for Denmark, Sweden, and the United States are shown in the fifth row of Table 9.1.[9]

Government services—medical care, child care, housing, transportation, and so on—reduce material hardship directly. They also free up income to be spent on other needs. The comparative data, though by no means perfect, are consistent with the hypothesis that public services help the poor more in the Nordic countries than in the United States. The gap between the countries in material deprivation is larger than in low-end incomes.

How is it that despite its greater social expenditures, the United States does less well by its poor than Denmark and Sweden? First, public cash and near-cash transfers in the United States are both smaller and less targeted (Figure 6.1) than in the Nordic countries. They therefore achieve less poverty reduction. Second, private transfers in the United States are large, but they consist mainly of employer contributions to employee retirement funds (company pensions and 401ks) and little of this money goes to the poor. Third, public services are less extensive in the United States. They certainly provide some benefit to the poor, but likely less than in Denmark and Sweden.[10] Fourth, private spending on services is quite hefty in the United States, but much of this money consists of employer contributions to private health insurance, and once again few among the poor are recipients.

CONCLUSION

Helping the poor is not the only thing we want from social spending. But it surely is one thing. The United States spends more money on social protection than is often thought, yet that spending does not do nearly as much to help America's poor as we might like. Gøsta Esping-Andersen once remarked, in the course of assessing the historical development of social protection programs, that "It is difficult to imagine that anyone struggled for spending per se."[11] The U.S. experience illustrates the sense in this.

10

Tradeoffs?

It often is said that there is no free lunch, that generosity comes at a cost. If we commit to improvement in the absolute living standards of the least well-off, must we sacrifice other desirable outcomes?

I offer only a preliminary analysis here. I conduct a broad but not particularly deep search for evidence that there might be some noteworthy drawback to helping the poor.

In Chapter 2 I showed a series of scatterplots that depicted the over-time relationship between GDP per capita and the incomes of low-end households in individual countries (Figure 2.1). We saw that in some countries economic growth produced rising incomes for the poor, whereas in others that was less true or not the case at all. One useful measure of improvement in the living standards of the least well-off is the slopes of the lines in those charts. They tell us the degree to which low-end household incomes rise as the society gets richer.

Another useful measure is a country's rate of material deprivation, as described in Chapter 4. Researchers from the OECD have computed a material deprivation rate that identifies the share of households experiencing one or more of the following: inability to adequately heat home, constrained food choices, overcrowding, poor environmental conditions (e.g., noise, pollution), arrears in payment of utility bills, arrears in mortgage or rent payment, difficulty in making ends meet. Unfortunately, these material deprivation rates are available at only a single point in time, the mid-2000s. They also do not include Canada or Switzerland, which reduces the number of countries from the seventeen that appear in Chapter 2 to fifteen.

I create a summary indicator of "progress for the poor" by combining the 1979–2007 tenth-percentile-income-by-GDP-per-capita slopes with the mid-2000s material deprivation rates.[1] Figure 10.1 displays a

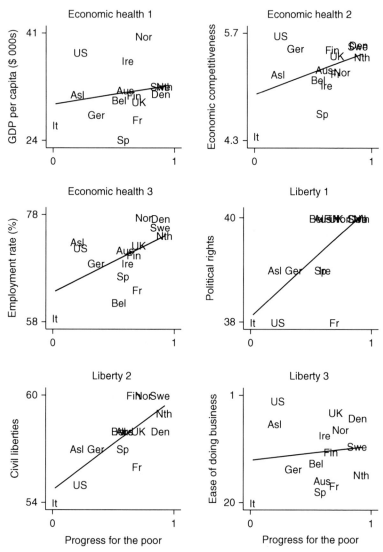

Figure 10.1. Is there evidence of tradeoffs between progress for the poor and other desirable outcomes?

Note: The values on the vertical axes are reversed in the sixth, eleventh, fourteenth, fifteenth, sixteenth, and twentieth charts. The "progress for the poor" measure on the horizontal axes is created by combining the slopes of the tenth-percentile-income-by-GDP-per-capita charts in Figure 2.1 with the material deprivation rates in Figure 4.1. For data definitions and sources, see the appendix.

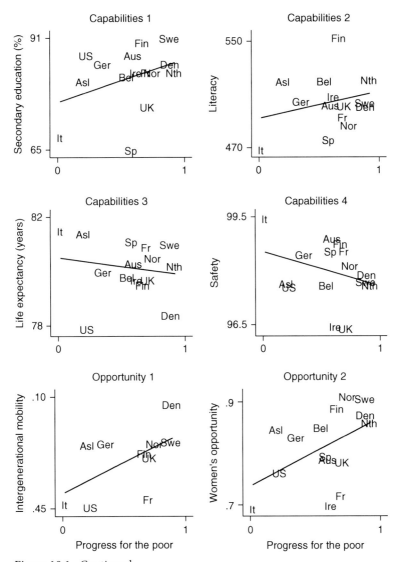

Figure 10.1. Continued

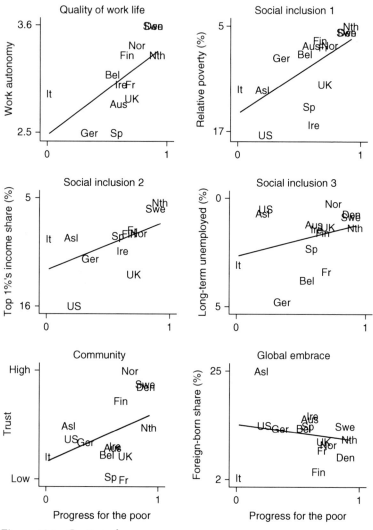

Figure 10.1. Continued

number of scatterplot graphs, each of which has this summary indicator on the horizontal axis. Countries positioned to the right have
been more successful at boosting the income of low-end households
and securing low rates of material deprivation.

What other outcomes might we desire? I consider ten: economic
health, liberty, capabilities, opportunity, quality of work life, social

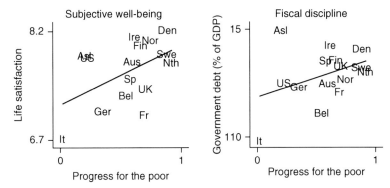

Figure 10.1. Continued

inclusion, community, global embrace, subjective well-being, and fiscal discipline. I use one or more indicators for each of them.[2] I aim for measurement in 2007, or as close to 2007 as possible. The year 2007 is the end of the period covered by the analyses in this book; it is the peak year in the 2000s business cycle, and predates the economic crash of 2008. The question is whether improving the absolute living standards of the poor has had adverse effects on other desirable outcomes, effects that should show up in measures of these outcomes at the end of the time period of interest. These outcome indicators are as follows:

- *Economic health 1*: GDP per capita.[3] This remains by far the most common measure of societal economic progress.[4]
- *Economic health 2*: economic competitiveness scores from the World Economic Forum. These aim to measure the quality of nine components of a nation's economy: public and private institutions, infrastructure, macroeconomic policy, health and primary education, higher education and training, market efficiency, technological readiness, business sophistication, and innovation.
- *Economic health 3*: the employment rate.[5]
- *Liberty 1*: political rights, as measured by the Freedom House.
- *Liberty 2*: civil liberties, as measured by the Freedom House.
- *Liberty 3*: the ease of starting a business, hiring and firing employees, and reaping the rewards of innovation, as judged by the World Bank.

- *Capabilities 1*: basic education, measured as the share of 25-to-34-year-olds that have completed upper secondary schooling or better.[6]

- *Capabilities 2*: literacy, measured as the average literacy score in math, science, and reading among 15-year-olds.

- *Capabilities 3*: life expectancy.

- *Capabilities 4*: safety, measured as the share of the population reporting that in the previous year they were not a victim of either a robbery or an assault or threatened assault.

- *Opportunity 1*: the degree of intergenerational mobility, as indicated by the weakness of the association between fathers' earnings and their sons' earnings.

- *Opportunity 2*: women's opportunity. The indicator is the United Nations Development Programme's measure of gender equality in politics and the economy. It is a composite of women's share of parliamentary seats, women's share of legislators, senior officials, and managers, women's share of professional and technical positions, and the ratio of female to male earned income.

- *Quality of work life*: work autonomy, measured as the average number of the following five aspects of the work process that employees report they are able to choose or change: the order of tasks, the methods of work, the speed of work, working partners, taking a break when desired.[7]

- *Social inclusion 1*: relative poverty, calculated as the share of people in households with an income less than 50% of the country median.[8]

- *Social inclusion 2*: the degree of inequality between the rich and the rest of the population, measured as the top 1%'s share of income.

- *Social inclusion 3*: the share of the labor force that has been unemployed for one year or longer.

- *Community*: the degree of interpersonal trust in a society, as suggested by the share responding "most people can be trusted" relative to the share responding "you can never be too careful when dealing with others."

- *Global embrace*: foreign-born share of the population.

- *Subjective well-being*: average life satisfaction, as indicated by responses on a 0–10 scale to the question "All things considered, how satisfied or dissatisfied are you with your life as a whole these days?"[9]
- *Fiscal discipline*: government debt as a share of GDP.[10]

The outcome measures are on the vertical axes of the charts in Figure 10.1. Each is arrayed so that higher on the vertical axis represents a better outcome. Evidence suggestive of a tradeoff therefore would appear in the form of a negatively sloped pattern.

The conclusion from these charts is straightforward: there is little or no indication that improvement in the absolute living standards of the poor entails a sacrifice of other valued outcomes.

Each of the twenty charts has a "best-fit" line that summarizes the pattern across the countries, and all but three of those lines are positively sloped. This suggests progress for the poor may be complementary to, rather than in conflict with, successful pursuit of these other outcomes.[11] But that is too strong a conclusion to draw from these simple plots. The conclusion here is more modest, though no less important: the empirical case for tradeoffs remains to be made.

11

The Politics of Helping the Poor

The analyses in Chapters 2–10 suggest the following lessons for affluent-country policy makers interested in improving the absolute living standards of the least well-off:

- Economic growth is vital for income growth of low-end households. But it is not sufficient. Growth reaches the least well-off principally via increases in government transfers. For most households, employment and earnings can and should be the chief trickle-down mechanism, but for many in the bottom decile transfers are the key.

- In a flexible labor market such as that of the United States, employment hours for the poorest may drop so much during business-cycle downturns that any gains achieved in the growth phase are nullified. Employment therefore cannot be the sole pillar on which antipoverty efforts rest.

- Low wages do not necessarily imply low household incomes. Programs such as an employment-conditional earnings subsidy coupled with a minimum wage can help nations that have a sizeable low-wage sector avoid high poverty. This may also serve as part of an approach to improve access to employment among immigrants and the young.

- Universalism in social policy can be beneficial for poverty reduction, but it is by no means necessary. Countries that make heavier use of targeting have tended to be as successful at income redistribution as those with less targeting.

- Public services are an important antipoverty tool. Their benefit does not show up in income data, but they appear to play a key role in reducing material deprivation. Services expand the sphere of consumption for which the cost is zero or minimal. And they help to boost the earnings and capabilities of the poor by enhancing human capital, assisting with job search and placement, and facilitating work–family balance.

- Taxes are important for antipoverty policy. But their contribution is indirect; taxes fund the transfers and services that are key to poverty reduction. Countries would do well to avoid heavy reliance on payroll taxes, but otherwise the structure of the tax system matters far less than the quantity of tax revenues generated.

- Spending lots of money on social protection is not in and of itself helpful to the poor. Total (public plus private) social expenditures in the United States are greater than in Denmark and Sweden, but far less of America's social spending reaches the poor.

- Tradeoffs are important to consider in designing social policy. The comparative evidence suggests, however, that improving the absolute living standards of the poor may require little or no sacrifice of other desirable goals.

If this constitutes a broad set of guidelines for an effective antipoverty strategy, how do countries get from here to there? Rather than attempt a general prescription, I will focus on the United States. The United States is by far the largest of these nations; it has a third of the total population of the twenty rich nations on which I have focused in this book. It also is, arguably, the nation with the longest road to travel. Its poor are not the worst off in an absolute sense (Chapters 2 and 4), but they fare much less well than they ought to given America's wealth.

Modest, regularized increases in America's statutory minimum wage, Earned Income Tax Credit (EITC), unemployment compensation, social assistance (TANF and Food Stamps), housing assistance, and public services such as health care and child care would yield significant reductions in income poverty and material deprivation.[1] Unfortunately, apart from a few exceptions, such as the EITC, movement in this direction has been halting. Why have the politics of helping America's poor proved so difficult?

WHAT SOCIAL SCIENCE TELLS US: STRUCTURES AND INSTITUTIONS RULE

Social scientists have been studying the determinants of social policy generosity for roughly four decades.[2] One key factor is the strength of organized labor and affiliated left political parties. Important too are the structure of the political system and decision-making processes, including whether the electoral system is proportional representation or majoritarian, the number and type of veto points, and the form of discussion and negotiation among policy makers, interest group representatives, and experts. Voter turnout seems to make a difference. Also relevant are economic and demographic pressures and constraints stemming from countries' degree of integration in the global economy, the unemployment rate, declines in manufacturing and agricultural employment, the age structure of the population, and the immigrant share.

This research aims to account for differences in social policy generosity across countries and over time. It tells us that a country with a weak labor movement or a majoritarian electoral system or a large number of veto points is less likely than countries with different institutions to have a generous welfare state. A nation with all three of these features, such as the United States, is especially unlikely to do so.

But tendencies are just that. To my knowledge, no influential study of social policy generosity in affluent countries has identified any necessary conditions either for the overall policy configuration or for particular programs. The world of social policy is not a deterministic one. Structures and institutions constrain, but they do not dictate outcomes.

Over the past half century, center-right Christian democratic parties have been nearly as important as social democratic ones in promoting generous social programs.[3] Government support for child care and early education in continental Belgium and France rivals that in social-democratic Denmark, Norway, and Sweden.[4] Employment-conditional earnings subsidies have been implemented and expanded in widely diverse institutional settings and by governments at all ends of the partisan spectrum.[5] By the same token, in recent decades we observe a number of significant reductions in the generosity of particular transfers or services under social democratic or other left governments: New Zealand and the Netherlands in the 1980s; Denmark, Sweden, and Canada in the 1990s; Germany in the early 2000s.

Given its political institutions—a privatized system of campaign financing, a federal government structure, extensive separation of powers within the federal government, a bicameral parliament, the filibuster practice in the Senate, and the lack of a truly left political party, among others—it is not surprising that America is a laggard in social policy generosity among the rich countries. Yet it was not foreordained that the United States would institute public health insurance programs for its elderly and its poor in the 1960s and enhance them in subsequent decades, expand its social assistance programs in the 1960s (AFDC) and 1970s (food stamps), create an employment-conditional earnings subsidy in the 1970s (the EITC) and expand it in subsequent decades, implement severe time limits on receipt of a key social assistance benefit (TANF) in the 1990s, or fail to adopt government support for near-universal health care coverage in the 1970s and 1990s but then pass it in 2010. The possibilities for American social policy surely are not endless. As one observer of the recent health-care reform battle has put it, "the institutional constraints on legislation . . . make enactment of sweeping legislation nightmarishly difficult."[6] But neither are prospects as limited as a focus on America's political structure might lead us to presume.

WHAT DOES THE AMERICAN PUBLIC WANT? AND DOES IT MATTER?

Do Americans want social programs that more effectively boost the incomes and material well-being of the poor? Several theories suggest they should.

The postmaterialist thesis, associated most closely with Ronald Inglehart, suggests that as societies grow more affluent citizens' preferences become increasingly disconnected from basic material needs.[7] People come to attach stronger priority to social justice and fairness. This should produce growing support for generous social programs. If we compare across rich and not-so-rich countries, the evidence is broadly consistent with this hypothesis: in cross-nationally comparable public opinion surveys such as the International Social Survey Program (ISSP) or the World Values Survey, the citizens in countries with higher per capita GDP tend to express greater support for programs that help the poor. But if we confine the comparison to the rich countries, the association between national wealth and public enthusiasm for a generous welfare state weakens considerably or disappears altogether. Moreover, if we look over time within the United States—at least in recent decades, which is the period for which regular data exist—we do not observe growing support for social policy generosity.[8]

A related view, offered by Benjamin Friedman, holds that generous attitudes are fostered by living standard *improvements*, rather than by high levels.[9] Being affluent is not enough, in other words; what is critical is that people feel they are moving ahead. Here too the U.S. experience is disappointing. Over the past several decades, GDP per capita has increased. So too has median income, though its growth has been slower than that of the economy as a whole. But as just noted, we observe no increase in attitudes favoring government efforts to help the poor.

The "median-voter" approach offers another optimistic hypothesis about public opinion and social policy generosity in countries such as the United States.[10] It contends that people's preference for redistribution is a straightforward function of their material interest in it. When market income inequality increases, the median voter becomes more likely to benefit from redistribution, since the difference between her tax payments and the benefits she receives tilts in favor of the latter. America has experienced a sharp increase in market inequality over the past generation, so this predicts a likely rise in public sentiment in favor of enhanced social policy generosity. Here too, however, a seemingly plausible theory does not fare well empirically. Public opinion surveys in the United States suggest that Americans recognize that income inequality has increased, but they do not indicate a consequent rise in support for redistributive efforts.[11] Nor does the theory seem to work in other countries for which over-time data are available.[12]

So what *do* Americans want? A generation of public opinion research, using both standard survey findings and more in-depth qualitative investigation, suggests the following.[13] Most Americans support capitalism and business. Many believe hard work, rather than luck or help from others, is the key to success. Many feel they have opportunity to get ahead. Many believe income inequality is too high and that high inequality is not necessary for the country's prosperity. At a general level, many are skeptical about government's ability to help. There is only limited support for enhanced redistribution as a remedy for high inequality. Yet Americans do support increased government spending on programs perceived to enhance opportunity and economic security.

A nontrivial share of Americans also favor increased government spending to help the poor.[14] Since the mid-1980s, 60–70 percent of those surveyed have said they agree "it is government's responsibility to take care of people who can't take care of themselves," and the same proportion has said government is "spending too little money on assistance to the poor." When asked if the government "should help more needy people even if it means going deeper into debt," 50 percent have tended to say yes.

In other words, Americans are potentially receptive to a more generous set of social programs, but their demand for it is far from overwhelming. The recent debate over legislation to reform the country's health insurance system is instructive. Public opinion polls show a steady rise in recent decades in the share of Americans saying the government is spending too little on the improving and protecting the nation's health, with the share reaching 75 percent by 2008.[15] Yet during the lengthy legislative debate on health-care reform, polls suggested lukewarm support at best for the type of bill that was finally passed.[16] Americans, in short, are ambivalent.

Is this an obstacle to enhanced social policy generosity? One view says yes: countries tend to get the level of social policy generosity their citizens support.[17] An alternative perspective suggests that this has the causality backwards: policy influences attitudes more than the other way around.[18] The public tends to support policies they perceive to be effective. Once generous programs get put in place, they build a constituency and become popular among the broad public. This makes backsliding difficult.[19] The key, therefore, is to get good programs enacted. Retrenchment can and will occur, in the form of cutbacks in eligibility, reductions in replacement rates, and so on. But over the past several decades it has proven difficult for policy makers in affluent countries to go very far down this road.[20]

A RAY OF HOPE

One of the most successful recent antipoverty efforts in affluent countries was that of the New Labour governments in the United Kingdom from 1997 to 2010. Though Tony Blair and Gordon Brown's governments focused much of their rhetoric and policy reform on increasing employment and economic opportunity, they also increased benefits and/or reduced taxes for low earners, single parents, and pensioners.[21] Tom Sefton, John Hills, and Holly Sutherland calculate that benefit and tax changes between 1997 and 2005 increased real disposable income for bottom-income-decile households by about 20 percent.[22] My calculations using data from the Luxembourg Income Study suggest a similar increase (Figure 2.2). It was one of the largest in any of the rich countries for which reliable data are available.

Blair and Brown did not initially campaign on an antipoverty platform. And there is little indication of demand among the British public for a surge in government generosity toward the poor. If anything, public support for redistribution and assistance to the poor was declining during the late 1990s.[23] Yet a year into New Labour's first term, the government made a commitment to end child poverty in the United Kingdom within a generation, and this led to a raft of policy initiatives that boosted incomes among Britain's poor.

American presidents and legislators with similar ambitions face different conditions. New Labour's efforts benefited from the fact that the United Kingdom's government has few veto points. When Blair and Brown made a commitment to reduce poverty, they faced fewer obstacles to following through on that commitment than an American president would. Still, over the course of the past century, U.S. policy makers sometimes have been able, even at unlikely moments, to fashion compromises that helped to boost the incomes and material well-being of America's low-end households.[24] This experience suggests reason for optimism—guarded, to be sure, but genuine—about prospects for the future.

Acknowledgments

I am grateful to my coauthors: Keith Bentele, Dan Duerr, and Jess Epstein. In addition to playing a key role in the development of the chapters on which their names appear, they each provided valuable comments on other parts of the book. Earlier versions of some of the chapters were presented at a variety of venues: the American Political Science Association annual meeting in 2010; the Harvard-Manchester Saguaro Seminar Summer Workshop in 2010; Indiana University in 2010; the "Inequality" conference at the University of Rome in 2008; the Juan March Institute in 2009; the Luxembourg Income Study conference on "Inequality and the Middle Class" in 2010; the Society for the Advancement of Socio-Economics annual meeting in 2004, 2005, and 2009; the Swedish Institute for Social Research in 2010; the University of Arizona Geography and Regional Development department in 2008; the University of Arizona Global Society and Justice workshop in 2008; the University of Arizona Sociology department in 2004 and 2007; the University of Washington Sociology department in 2009; the "Wealth and Power in the Postindustrial Age" workshops at Yale and UCLA in 2005 and 2008. I thank the many participants and discussants.

I also appreciate helpful comments and suggestions from Bruce Bradbury, Andrea Brandolini, Tommy Ferrarini, Nancy Folbre, Steffen Ganghof, Andrew Gelman, Anton Hemerijck, Alex Hicks, Markus Jantti, Christopher Jencks, Jan Jonsson, Ollie Kangas, Tomas Korpi, Walter Korpi, Vince Mahler, Ive Marx, John Myles, Kenneth Nelson, Brian Nolan, Joakim Palme, Jonas Pontusson, Robert Putnam, Bo Rothstein, David Rueda, Michael Shalev, and Bruce Western.

Parts of the book were written during stints as a visiting scholar at the Juan March Institute in Madrid, the Amsterdam Centre for Inequality Studies at the University of Amsterdam, and the Swedish Institute for Social Research (SOFI) at Stockholm University. I am grateful to Andrew Richards, Herman van de Werfhorst, Jelle Visser, and Tomas Korpi, who initiated and organized these visits.

I want to thank Dominic Byatt at Oxford University Press, along with Oxford's fine editorial and production staff.

My most important thanks go to my family: Kim, Mia, Hannah, Noah, and Josh. In ways small and large, they make my life a treasure.

APPENDIX

Data Definitions and Sources

The data used in this book are available at www.u.arizona.edu/~lkenwor.

COUNTRIES

Asl	Australia	Ja	Japan
Aus	Austria	Nth	The Netherlands
Bel	Belgium	NZ	New Zealand
Can	Canada	Nor	Norway
Den	Denmark	Por	Portugal
Fin	Finland	Sp	Spain
Fr	France	Swe	Sweden
Ger	Germany	Swi	Switzerland
Ire	Ireland	UK	The United Kingdom
It	Italy	US	The United States

C&P tax share. Consumption and payroll tax revenues as a share of total tax revenues. *Source*: Author's calculations using data from OECD 2010.

Capabilities 1: secondary education. Share of persons age 25–34 that have completed upper secondary education or better. Measured in 2007. *Source*: OECD 2009a: Table A1.2a.

Capabilities 2: literacy. Average PISA literacy score in math, science, and reading among 15-year-olds. Measured in 2006. *Source*: OECD 2010.

Capabilities 3: life expectancy. Life expectancy at birth. Measured in 2007. *Source*: OECD 2010.

Capabilities 4: safety. Share of the population reporting that in the previous year they were not a victim of either a robbery or an assault or threatened assault. Measured in 2004. *Source*: van Dijk, van Kesteren, and Smit 2007: Tables 11–13.

Community: trust. Index: 100 + (share of responding saying "most people can be trusted" − share responding "you can never be too careful when dealing with others"). Measured in 1999–2005. *Source*: Medrano 2010, using World Values Survey data.

Consumption tax share. Consumption tax revenues as a share of total tax revenues. *Source*: Author's calculations using data from OECD 2010.

Economic health 1: GDP per capita. Gross domestic product per person. In year-2000 U.S. dollars, with currencies converted using purchasing power parities. Measured in 2007. *Source*: Author's calculations using data from OECD 2010.

Economic health 2: economic competitiveness. Index that aims to assess the quality of nine components of a nation's economy: public and private institutions, infrastructure, macroeconomic policy, health and primary education, higher education and training, market efficiency, technological readiness, business sophistication, and innovation. The index ranges from a low of 1 to a high of 7. Measured in 2007–8. *Source*: World Economic Forum 2008.

Economic health 3: employment rate. Employed persons as a share of the population age 15–64. Measured in 2007. *Source*: OECD 2010.

Education. Average years of schooling completed among the population age 25 and over. *Source*: Barro and Lee n.d.

Employment. Employed persons as a share of the population age 15–64. *Source*: Author's calculations using data from OECD 2010.

Employment in agriculture. Employed persons in agriculture as a share of the population age 15–64. *Source*: Author's calculations using data from OECD 2010.

Employment in manufacturing. Employed persons in manufacturing as a share of the population age 15–64. *Source*: Author's calculations using data from OECD 2010.

Fiscal discipline: government debt. General government gross financial liabilities as a share of GDP. *Source*: OECD 2010.

GDP per capita. Gross domestic product (GDP) per capita, adjusted for inflation and converted into U.S. dollars using purchasing power parities (PPPs). *Source*: Author's calculations using data from OECD 2010.

Global embrace: foreign-born share of the population. Source: OECD 2010.

Government transfers per person. Government transfers per capita. The data include public spending on old age, survivors, incapacity-related benefits, family, unemployment, and "other." *Source*: Author's calculations using data from OECD 2010.

Imports. Imports as a share of GDP. *Source*: Author's calculations using data from OECD 2010.

Inequality reduction via government services. Gini coefficient for posttransfer-posttax income minus Gini coefficient for posttransfer-posttax income plus imputed value of public services. *Source*: Marical et al. 2006: Annex Table A.9.

Inequality reduction via government transfers. Gini coefficient for pretransfer-pretax income minus Gini coefficient for posttransfer-pretax income.

Incomes are adjusted for household size using the square root of the number of persons in the household as the equivalence scale, top-coded at 10 times the unequivalized median, and bottom-coded at 1 percent of the equivalized mean. *Source*: Author's calculations using data from LIS 2010*a*.

Inequality reduction via taxes. Gini coefficient for pretransfer-pretax income minus Gini coefficient for pretransfer-posttax income. Incomes are adjusted for household size using the square root of the number of persons in the household as the equivalence scale, top-coded at 10 times the unequivalized median, and bottom-coded at 1 percent of the equivalized mean. *Source*: Author's calculations using data from LIS 2010*a*.

Liberty 1: political rights. Sum of Freedom House scores for three items: electoral process, political pluralism and participation, and functioning of government. Measured in 2007. *Source*: Freedom House 2007.

Liberty 2: civil liberties. Sum of Freedom House scores for four items: freedom of expression and belief, associational and organizational rights, rule of law, and personal autonomy and individual rights. Measured in 2007. *Source*: Freedom House 2007.

Liberty 3: ease of doing business. Each country is scored in five areas: the cost of starting a business (percentage of income per capita), the cost of registering property, the difficulty of hiring employees (index), the difficulty of firing employees (index), the cost of enforcing contracts (percentage of debt). These scores are aggregated and the countries are rank-ordered. Measured in 2005. *Source*: World Bank 2007: Table 1.2.

Low-end incomes. Tenth-percentile (P10) household income per equivalent person. Incomes are adjusted for inflation and converted into year-2000 U.S. dollars using PPPs, adjusted for household size using the square root of the number of persons in the household as the equivalence scale, top-coded at 10 times the unequivalized median, and bottom-coded at 1 percent of the equivalized mean. *Source*: Author's calculations using household income data from LIS 2010*a* (variable: DPI) and inflation and PPP data from OECD 2010.

Material deprivation. Average share of respondents reporting deprivation as of the mid-2000s in seven areas: inability to adequately heat home, constrained food choices, overcrowding, poor environmental conditions, arrears in payments of utility bills, arrears in mortgage or rent payments, and difficulty making ends meet. *Source*: OECD 2008: 186–8, using data from the Survey on Income and Living Conditions (EU-SILC) for European countries, the Household Income and Labour Dynamics in Australia survey (HILDA) for Australia, and the Survey of Income and Program Participation (SIPP) for the United States.

Opportunity 1: intergenerational income mobility. Strength of association between fathers' earnings and their sons' earnings. *Source*: Björklund and Jantti 2009: Figure 20.1.

Opportunity 2: women's opportunity. A composite measure of women's share of parliamentary seats, women's share of legislators, senior officials, and managers, women's share of professional and technical positions, and the ratio of female to male earned income. Measured in 2000–7. *Source*: UNDP 2007: Table 29 ("gender empowerment").

Progress for the poor. Combination of the slopes in the tenth-percentile-income-by-GDP-per-capita charts in Figure 2.1 with the material deprivation rates in Figure 4.1. Each of these is rescaled to vary from 0 to 1 and then they are averaged.

Quality of work life: work autonomy. Average number of the following five aspects of the work process that employees report they are able to choose or change: the order of tasks, the methods of work, the speed of work, working partners, take a break when desired. Excludes the self-employed. The data are available for European countries only. Measured in 2005. *Source*: Eurofound 2007: Figure 6.1.

Redistribution. Degree of inequality reduction relative to the degree of market inequality. Calculated as: ((pretransfer-pretax Gini coefficient − posttransfer-posttax Gini)/pretransfer-pretax Gini) × 100. *Source*: Author's calculations using data from LIS 2010*a*.

Social inclusion 1: relative poverty rate. Share of persons in households with size-adjusted posttransfer-posttax income less than 50 percent of the country median. Measured in 2000–5. *Source*: LIS 2010*b*.

Social inclusion 2: top 1 percent's income share. Share of pretax income (excluding capital gains) going to the top 1 percent of taxpaying units. Measured in 2000. *Source*: Atkinson, Piketty, and Saez 2009.

Social inclusion 3: long-term unemployed. Share of the labor force unemployed for twelve months or longer. Measured in 2007. *Source*: OECD 2010.

Social policy generosity. Government social expenditures as a share of GDP, adjusted for the share of the population age 65 and over and for the unemployment rate. The adjustment is as follows: adjusted government social expenditures = government social expenditures + (0.5 × (21 − (elderly share of the population + unemployment rate))). (This implies that each percentage point of the elderly share and/or unemployment costs about 0.5 percent of GDP. Twenty-one is the average across all countries and years for the elderly share plus the unemployment rate.) The data include public spending on transfers and services in nine areas of social policy: old age, survivors, incapacity-related benefits, health, family, active labor market programs, unemployment, housing, and "other." *Source*: Author's calculations using data from OECD 2010.

Subjective well-being: life satisfaction. Country mean for responses to the question "All things considered, how satisfied or dissatisfied are you with your life as a whole these days?" Possible range of scores is 0–10. Measured in 2008. *Source*: Veenhoven 2010, using World Gallup Poll data.

Targeting-universalism. Index of concentration, which equals −1 if the household with the lowest pretransfer-pretax income gets all of the government transfer income, 0 if all persons get an equal amount of transfer income, and +1 if the household with the highest pretransfer-pretax income gets all of the transfer income. Included are the following types of public transfers: pension benefits, child and family allowances, unemployment compensation, sick pay, accident pay, disability pay, maternity pay, military/veterans/war benefits, "other social insurance," means-tested cash benefits, and "near-cash" benefits. *Source*: Author's calculations using data from LIS 2010*a*.

Tax revenues. Government tax revenues as a share of GDP. *Source*: OECD 2010.

Tax revenues: consumption taxes. Government revenues from taxes on goods and services as a share of GDP. *Source*: OECD 2010.

Tax revenues: income taxes. Government revenues from taxes on income and profits as a share of GDP. *Source*: OECD 2010.

Tax revenues: payroll taxes. Government revenues from social security contributions and payroll taxes as a share of GDP. *Source*: OECD 2010.

Unemployment. Unemployed persons as a share of the labor force. *Source*: OECD 2010.

Unionization. Union members (minus retired workers, independent workers, students, and unemployed workers) as a share of wage and salary earners in employment. *Source*: Visser 2009 (variable: UD).

Wage-bargaining coverage. Share of employees whose wages are determined by collective bargaining. *Source*: Visser 2009 (variable: ADJCOV).

U.S. STATES

Education. Persons age 25–64 with less than a high school degree as a share of all persons age 25–64. *Source*: Authors' calculations using data from the Current Population Survey (NBER MORG Extracts).

Employment. Employed persons age 25–64 as a share of the population age 25–64. *Source*: Authors' calculations using Current Population Survey data (IPUMS March Extracts; see King et al. 2004).

Employment hours in low-end households. Average annual hours worked in working-age ("head" age 25–64) households in the bottom quartile of the pretransfer-pretax income distribution. *Source:* Authors' calculations using data from the Current Population Survey (IPUMS March Extracts; see King et al. 2004).

Female-headed households. Persons in households with a single female adult age 25–64 as a share of persons in all households with a "head" age 25–64. *Source:* Authors' calculations using data from the Current Population Survey (IPUMS March Extracts; see King et al. 2004).

Gross state product (GSP) per capita. Adjusted for inflation using the CPI-U-RS. *Source:* Authors' calculations using GSP and population data from the Bureau of Economic Analysis and inflation data from the Bureau of Labor Statistics.

Low-end hourly wages. Hourly wage at the tenth percentile of the distribution, adjusted for inflation using the CPI-U-RS. Sample includes wage and salary workers age 16–64 with positive potential experience. This excludes self-employed individuals and those with negative potential experience, where potential is defined as respondent's age minus years of education minus 6. In the CPS, workers paid by the hour are asked directly about their hourly rate of pay. This response is used as the hourly wage measure for this group of workers. For non-hourly workers, the hourly wage is computed by dividing usual weekly earnings by usual hours per week. *Source:* Authors' calculations using wage data from the Current Population Survey data (IPUMS March Extracts; see King et al. 2004) and inflation data from the Bureau of Labor Statistics.

Low-end market incomes. Tenth-percentile (P10) pretransfer-pretax household income per equivalent person. Incomes are adjusted for inflation using the CPI-U-RS and adjusted for household size using the square root of the number of persons in the household as the equivalence scale. Households with a "head" age 25–59. *Source:* Authors' calculations using income data from the Current Population Survey data (IPUMS March Extracts; see King et al. 2004) and inflation data from the Bureau of Labor Statistics.

Unemployment. Unemployed persons as a share of the labor force. *Source:* Bureau of Labor Statistics.

Notes

CHAPTER 1

1. Rawls 1971.
2. I disagree with part of Rawls's argument. If a rise in inequality is very large, it may be objectionable despite an absolute improvement for the poor. See Kenworthy 2008b: ch. 2.
3. In experiments in which five or so participants are placed in a situation approximating Rawls's original position, most do not choose his distributive principle. Instead, they tend to choose a principle in which the average income is maximized with a floor under the incomes of those at the bottom. See Frohlich, Oppenheimer, and Eavey 1987.
4. Friedman 2005.
5. Citro and Michael 1995; Atkinson et al. 2002, 2005; Rainwater and Smeeding 2003; Brady 2009.
6. This is true when comparing across countries as well. For example, Mexico and Russia have relative poverty rates only slightly higher than the United States, and the rates in Poland and Romania are far lower than in the United States; see LIS 2010b. Because the U.S. median income is comparatively high, 50 percent of its median is high, resulting in a fairly large share of American households having income below that cutoff. In Poland, Romania, Russia, and Mexico, by contrast, the median income is comparatively low, so the poverty line ends up being quite low. Similarly, the level of relative poverty in Mississippi is the same as in Connecticut; see Iceland, Kenworthy, and Scopolitti 2005; Burkhauser 2009.
7. Kenworthy 2008a; Nolan 2008.
8. See Chapter 4. Also Slesnick 2001; Haveman and Wolff 2005; Meyer and Sullivan 2009; Garfinkel, Rainwater, and Smeeding 2010.
9. Even direct measures of living standards miss something important. Though I do not pursue it further in this book, I share Amartya Sen's view that antipoverty efforts should aim not just at securing improved material well-being but also at enhancing people's capabilities. By this Sen means the ability to develop informed preferences about life goals and to act on those preferences. Income is a key resource that increases one's capability. But there are many others: education, physical health, safety, employment, the freedom to start a business, to engage in trade, to participate in social life, and so on. Government has an important role

to play here, particularly via provision of services. See Sen 1992, 1999; Robeyns 2005; Nussbaum 2006.

CHAPTER 2

1. Dollar and Kraay 2002: 219.
2. Rodrik 2007: 2.
3. Firebaugh and Beck 1994; Chen and Ravallion 2001; Dollar and Kraay 2002 Collier 2007; Rodrik 2007; Commission on Growth and Development 2008. For a contrasting view, see UNRISD 2010.
4. Goodin et al. 1999; Smeeding, Rainwater, and Burtless 2001; Kangas 2002; Moller et al. 2003; Smeeding 2006; Bäckman 2009; Brady 2009.
5. Lyle Scruggs and James Allan find that higher GDP per capita is associated with lower absolute poverty rates in sixteen nations during the 1980s and 1990s. See Scruggs and Allan 2006.
6. Social scientists and policy researchers typically use a poverty rate measure, whether absolute or relative. A limitation of this strategy as a means of gauging the material well-being of those at the low end of the distribution is that a poverty rate identifies only the share of the population that is below the poverty line. It conveys no information about the depth or severity of poverty among those classified as poor; see Sen 1976; Citro and Michael 1995; Brady 2009. I instead compare income levels among households at a common spot in the bottom part of the income distribution: the tenth percentile (P10). This follows Kenworthy 2004: ch. 6; Brandolini and Smeeding 2006. The tenth percentile is a common reference point in analyses of income distributions. A frequently used measure of inequality, for instance, is the ratio of the income at the ninetieth percentile to the income at the tenth (P90/P10 ratio).

   An alternative is to multiply the poverty rate by the poverty gap, with the latter defined as the distance between the poverty line and the average income among the poor; see Atkinson 1987; Osberg and Xu 2000; OECD 2008; Brady 2009. These two approaches are very similar in practice; see Kenworthy 2004: ch. 6.

   Some will object that a household at the tenth percentile of the income distribution in countries such as Norway and Denmark is not really "poor." And according to the conventional relative approach to poverty, that is true; see LIS 2010b. My interest is in those at the low end of the distribution in each country. I use "the poor" as shorthand for that group.
7. LIS 2010a; Atkinson and Brandolini 2001; Saunders 2010.
8. This is standard practice. The adjustment presumes economies of scale within households; for instance, a household with four people is assumed to need twice as much income as a household of one, rather than four times as much. I use the LIS equivalence scale: the square root

of the number of persons in the household. The numbers on the vertical axes in the charts in Figure 2.1 refer to income "per equivalent person." They represent income for a household with a single adult; for a household of four, multiply by two.

9. In the other five countries—Austria, Belgium, France, Italy, and Spain—earnings cannot be separated from taxes.

10. This reinforces prior findings that government transfers are critical to poverty alleviation. See also Blank 1997*a*; Kenworthy 1999, 2004: ch. 6, 2010*a*; Smeeding 2005, 2006; Palme 2006; Marx and Verbist 2008*a*; Moffitt and Scholz 2009; OECD 2009*b*.

11. On Sweden see also Björklund and Freeman 2010; Jonsson, Mood, and Bihagen 2010.

12. See also Sefton, Hills, and Sutherland 2009; Waldfogel 2010.

13. Moffitt and Scholz 2009.

14. See also Picot, Morissette, and Myles 2003; Saunders and Bradbury 2006; Bosch and Weinkopf 2008.

15. The data for Germany are for West Germany prior to 1990 and for unified Germany thereafter.

16. Author's calculations using LIS data.

17. Is the finding that net government transfers have driven increases in the absolute incomes of low-end households due to over-time compositional shifts? Is it, for instance, a function of population aging, with some countries experiencing a rising number of elderly households relative to working-age households? No; the share of bottom-income-decile households with a "head" age 60 or over remained relatively constant in most of the countries over time. The chief exception is Ireland, as noted in the text.

18. Esping-Andersen 1999; Esping-Andersen et al. 2002; Scharpf and Schmidt 2000; Kenworthy 2004, 2008*b*, 2009*e*; OECD 2005, 2006; Pontusson 2005; Hemerijck 2012.

19. Kenworthy 2008*b*: Figure 3.4.

20. See also Freeman 2002.

21. Government social expenditures as a share of GDP rose in many, but that was largely a function of increases in spending on services, particularly health care. See OECD 2010.

22. See Figure 4.3.

23. Is the pattern due to a "catch-up" process? Is it countries in which the incomes of low-end households were comparatively low in 1979 that have increased their transfers more in order to help growth trickle down more to the poor? No; there is no association to speak of between the level of tenth-percentile incomes early in the period I am examining and the low-end-incomes-by-GDP-per-capita slopes in the charts in Figure 2.1.

CHAPTER 3

1. Prior research has focused mainly on wages. See Blank and Blinder 1986; Sawhill 1988; Blank and Card 1993; Blank 1997*b*; Haveman and Schwabisch 2000; Freeman 2001; DeFina 2002; Iceland 2003; Gundersen and Ziliak 2004. Exceptions include Iceland, Kenworthy, and Scopilliti 2005; Blank, Danziger, and Schoeni 2006.

2. The exceptions are Nebraska, North Dakota, and South Dakota.

3. No control variables are needed. As a matter of simple arithmetic, most of the change in pretransfer-pretax incomes of low-end households must come from either changes in employment hours or changes in earnings per employment hour. There are other sources of market income, such as alimony, child support, and private pensions; but as the United States chart in Figure 2.2 indicates, these are both minor in quantity and largely constant over time.

4. Mishel, Bernstein, and Shierholz 2009: ch. 4. See also Figure 3.4.

5. The 1997 shift from AFDC to TANF changed this.

6. Goldin and Katz 2008: 329–35.

7. Our calculations using CPS data.

8. Kenworthy 2008*b*.

9. Wright and Dwyer 2003: 304.

10. This story is quite different from other accounts. Rebecca Blank, for instance, attributes the failure of economic growth to reduce poverty in the 1980s and 1990s largely to stagnant wages and changes in household composition. See Blank 1997*a*: 222–3.

11. Murray 1984.

12. Blank 2002, 2006; Jencks 2005; Myles et al. 2009.

13. An additional problem for the social-policy-is-to-blame hypothesis is that social assistance benefits in the United States—mainly AFDC/ TANF and food stamps—have never been particularly generous; see Edin and Lein 1997. Moreover, their value has decreased steadily since the mid-1970s; see Jencks 1992; Blank 1997*a*; Nelson 2004.

14. Baumol, Blinder, and Wolff 2003.

15. Reber and Tyson 2004.

16. Freeman and Rodgers 2005.

17. Across states, there is a relatively strong correlation between wages and household market incomes at any given point in time. Apart from a few exceptions, such as Massachusetts and New York, a state's P10 household income level tends to correspond to its P10 hourly wage level. Our interest here, though, is in the over-time trends.

18. Blank 2000; Freeman 2001; Mishel et al. 2009.

19. Bernstein and Baker 2003; Mishel et al. 2009.

20. OECD 1994; Krugman 1996; Blau and Kahn 2002; Howell 2005.

21. Mishel et al. 2009.
22. Goldin and Katz 2008; Mishel et al. 2009.
23. Figure 2.2; Kenworthy 2008*b*: ch. 5.
24. Blank 2000, 2009; Ellwood 2000; Meyer and Sullivan 2009; Meyer and Wallace 2009.

CHAPTER 4

1. Townsend 1979; Mayer and Jencks 1989.
2. Mack and Lansley 1985; Gordon and Pantazis 1997; Gordon et al. 2000.
3. Beverly 2001*a*; USBC 2003; U.S. Department of Health and Human Services 2004; Short 2005; Iceland and Bauman 2007.
4. Ringen 1988; Callan, Nolan, and Whelan 1993; Halleröd 1995, 1996; Nolan and Whelan 1996.
5. Mayer 1993, 1995; Edin and Lein 1997; Rector et al. 1999; Burchardt 2000; Layte et al. 2001; Whelan et al. 2001, 2002, 2003, 2004; Palme et al. 2002; Perry 2002; Bradshaw and Finch 2003; Dekkers 2003; Muffels and Fourage 2004; Rector and Johnson 2004; Boarini and Mira d'Ercole 2006; OECD 2008: ch. 7; Alkire and Santos 2010; Nolan and Whelan 2010.
6. Layte et al. 2001; OECD 2008: ch. 7.
7. Most find only moderate overlap between those with low income and those who suffer material deprivation. See Mayer and Jencks 1989; Callan, Nolan, and Whelan 1993; Nolan and Whelan 1996; Gordon and Pantazis 1997; Beverly 2001*b*; Boushey et al. 2001; Perry 2002; Whelan, Layte, and Maître 2002, 2003, 2004; Bradshaw and Finch 2003; Muffels and Fourage 2004; Rector and Johnson 2004; Teitler et al. 2004; U.S. Department of Health and Human Services 2004; Saunders and Adelman 2005; Short 2005; Boarini and Mira d'Ercole 2006; Iceland and Bauman 2007; Sullivan, Turner, and Danziger 2008.
8. OECD 2008: 189.
9. The correlation is 0.99. Marlier et al. 2009 create a similar measure of the share deprived on three or more of nine items, using EU-SILC data for 2006. Across the thirteen EU countries included in both measures, the two measures correlate at 0.87.
10. The "deprivation line"—the cutoff used to classify a household as materially deprived or not—is the same across nations.
11. Lebergott 1976; Cox and Alm 1999; DeLong 2009.
12. Layte, Nolan, and Whelan 2000; Whelan, Nolan, and Maître 2007. Relatedly, Boarini and Mira d'Ercole find that across the full set of OECD countries, including the less affluent (mainly central and east European) ones, there is a fairly strong negative bivariate association

between per capita GDP and material deprivation; see OECD 2008: ch. 7.

13. See Boarini and Mira d'Ercole 2006: 18.
14. Nolan and Whelan 2010.
15. See the appendix for details. We decided against two alternative measures of social policy generosity. One is the difference between pretransfer-pretax income inequality and posttransfer-posttax income inequality (Bradley et al. 2003; Kenworthy and Pontusson 2005; Mahler and Jesuit 2006). The other is a measure of decommodification (Esping-Andersen 1990; Scruggs and Allan 2006)—a composite indicator of eligibility rules, benefit duration, and benefit levels for unemployment compensation, sickness compensation, and old-age pensions. Each of these measures has merit. But both have a significant drawback: they do not include government services. Like transfers, public services are redistributive and improve the living standards of the poor. (Also problematic for the decommodification measure is that it includes only three programs.) For more discussion of the strengths and weaknesses of these measures, see Bergh 2005; Castles 2008; Adema and Ladaique 2009; Garfinkel, Rainwater, and Smeeding 2010.
16. This association remains strong with controls for GDP per capita, education, unemployment, employment in agriculture, and imports.

CHAPTER 5

1. Bosch and Weinkopf 2008; Gautié and Schmitt 2010.
2. Visser 2006; Eurofound 2009.
3. See Kenworthy 2009c; Visser 2009.
4. Gautié and Schmitt 2010.
5. Venn 2009.
6. It is not only the political right that has favored policy changes to promote expansion of low-wage employment. In Germany, mini-jobs and the Hartz reforms were key developments; both were implemented by a Social Democratic government. In the Netherlands a central part of the story is the slow but steady drop in the statutory minimum wage, which was part of a compromise to which the union confederations and Social Democratic party policy makers assented; see Visser and Hemerijck 1997.
7. Gautié and Schmitt 2010.
8. Marx and Verbist 1998; Nolan and Marx 2000; Bardone and Guio 2005; Andreß and Lohmann 2008.
9. Gießelmann and Lohmann 2008; Halleröd and Larsson 2008; Lohmann 2008; Lohmann and Marx 2008; Marx and Verbist 2008b; Snel, de Boom, and Engbersen 2008; Whiteford and Adema 2008; OECD 2009.

10. See also Kenworthy 2004: ch. 6.
11. OECD 2009*b*.
12. Blank, Card, and Robbins 2000; Hoffman and Seidman 2003; Hotz and Scholz 2004.
13. Immervoll and Pearson 2009.
14. Kenworthy 2008*b*: ch. 7.
15. Immervoll and Pearson 2009: 16.
16. Immervoll and Pearson 2009: Table 3.
17. Ehrenreich 2001; Thompson 2010.
18. Gallie 2003; Kenworthy 2008*b*: 308–10.
19. Gallie 2002.
20. Esping-Andersen 1999, 2009; Esping-Andersen et al. 2002; Andersson, Holzer, and Lane 2005; Fitzgerald 2006.
21. Herzenberg, Alic, and Wial 1998.
22. Pontusson 2011.
23. E.g., Hall and Soskice 2001; Hall and Gingerich 2004; Barth and Moene 2009.
24. Streeck 2009.
25. Kenworthy 2006; Campbell and Pedersen 2007.
26. Kenworthy 2008*b*: Table 7.2.
27. Rothstein 1998.
28. Goodin et al. 1999.
29. Blank 1997*a*; Currie 2006; CAPTFP 2007; Haskins and Sawhill 2009.

CHAPTER 6

1. Esping-Andersen 1999; Scharpf and Schmidt 2000; Huber and Stephens 2001; Pierson 2001*b*; Kenworthy 2004, 2008*b*; OECD 2005, 2006; Hemerijck 2012.
2. Blank 1997*a*: ch. 6; Gilbert 2002: ch. 5; Schuck and Zeckhauser 2006.
3. Wilensky 1975; Korpi 1980; Rainwater 1982; Ringen 1987; Esping-Andersen 1990; Skocpol 1991; Gelbach and Pritchett 1995; Korpi and Palme 1998; Rothstein 1998; Moene and Wallerstein 2001; van Oorschot 2002; Pontusson 2005; Campbell 2007; Larsen 2008.
4. Korpi and Palme 1998; Kim 2000; Pontusson 2005.
5. Korpi and Palme 1998: 672.
6. Korpi and Palme 1998: 663.
7. Korpi and Palme 1998: 677.
8. LIS 2010*a*.
9. This is similar to a measure used by Korpi and Palme 1998: Table 3.
10. Howard 2007; Alber 2010.
11. Whiteford 2008, 2009.

12. Note that this reduces the estimated degree of redistribution; compare the vertical axis values in Figure 6.2 to those in Figure 6.1. It also allows some countries to have "reverse targeting," whereby more government transfers go to households with high incomes than to those with low incomes; compare the horizontal axis values in Figure 6.2 to those in Figure 6.1.
13. Atkinson and Brandolini 2001.
14. Greenstein 1991.
15. Pierson 1994.
16. Howard 2007: 106.
17. Nelson 2007: Figure 1.
18. See van Oorschot 2002; Matsaganis et al. 2004; de Neubourg, Castonguay, and Roelen 2007; Rothstein 2010.

CHAPTER 7

1. OECD 2008: ch. 9; Garfinkel, Rainwater, and Smeeding 2010: Table 4.1; Paulus, Sutherland, and Tsakloglou 2010.
2. Kenworthy 2009*a*, 2009*b*.
3. OECD 2008: ch. 9.
4. Goldin and Katz 2008; Garfinkel, Rainwater, and Smeeding 2010.
5. Kozol 1991.
6. Hoxby 2003.
7. Currie 2006.
8. OECD 2008: Figure 9.4.
9. Gornick and Meyers 2003; Huo, Nelson, and Stephens 2008; Kenworthy 2008*b*; Esping-Andersen and Myles 2009; Pontusson 2011; Hemerijck 2012.

CHAPTER 8

1. Warren 2008; Prasad and Deng 2009.
2. Ringen 1987: ch. 8; Mitchell 1991; Steinmo 1993; Mahler and Jesuit 2006; Kenworthy 2008*b*.
3. LIS 2010*a*.
4. Information on consumption taxes paid is very difficult to capture accurately in surveys.
5. Wilensky 1976, 2002: ch. 10; Becker and Mulligan 2003; Kato 2003; Cusack and Beramendi 2006; Beramendi and Rueda 2007; Kemmerling 2009.
6. Becker and Mulligan 2003.
7. Ganghof 2005, 2006, 2007.
8. This is not a function of beginning in 1960. Starting in 1973 or 1979 does not yield a different story.

9. How did previous analyses miss this? As best I can tell, two factors probably contributed. First, Becker and Mulligan and Kato estimated regressions that include a variety of control variables. The question of interest here is: Have countries that increased tax revenues in recent years done so mainly by increasing consumption and payroll taxes? To answer this question it is not necessary to estimate a multivariate regression model; this is an accounting question, not a question about causality. It may be that the addition of controls, such as political partisanship and globalization, hid the lack of over-time association between tax revenues and the tax mix.

Second, Becker and Mulligan and Kato each pooled cross-sectional with over-time data. Because the cross-country variation is more pronounced than the longitudinal variation, it is possible that in those pooled analyses the positive association across countries (see Figure 8.5) masked the lack of positive association over time (Figure 8.6). (This is common in macrocomparative analysis. See Griffin et al. 1986; Kittel 1999; Kenworthy 2007, 2009d; Shalev 2007.)

In addition to her quantitative analysis, Kato examined developments in the tax mix in several individual countries. However, the principal country she looked at that significantly increased tax revenues over time is Sweden, which turns out to be one of only two countries whose experience conforms to her hypothesis. Had she included Austria, Belgium, Denmark, Finland, or Italy among her case studies, she might have reached a different conclusion. Kato (2003: 94–110) did examine France, which experienced a rise in tax revenues without any increase in the share accounted for by consumption and payroll taxes. But it does not appear that she looked closely at over-time developments in the tax mix. Instead, her discussion focuses on changes in France's tax rates for payroll and consumption. Ganghof (2006: 364) notes that increasing income (and property) tax revenues played an important role in France.

10. Korpi 1985; Atkinson 1999; Lindert 2004: chs. 10, 18.
11. Slemrod and Bakija 2004: ch. 4; Myles 2009. Some studies that add a group of moderate-tax high-growth countries have found a negative association between taxation and economic growth. See Fölster and Henrekson 2001; Bergh and Karlsson 2010.
12. Lindert 2004: 235–45.
13. Scharpf 1997.
14. Scharpf 2000; Kemmerling 2005, 2009; OECD 2007; Kenworthy 2008b.
15. Kenworthy 2008b: ch. 8.
16. Visser 2002; Kenworthy 2008b: ch. 4.
17. Esping-Andersen 1990; Palier and Martin 2007.
18. Palier and Martin 2007; Hemerijck and Eichhorst 2009.
19. Palier 2000.

20. Streeck 2009: ch. 4.
21. Palier and Martin 2007; Rueda 2007.
22. See also Ganghof 2006.

CHAPTER 9

1. Adema 2001; Adema and Ladaique; 2009; Fishback 2010. See also Adema 1997; Howard 1997, 2007; Hacker 2002; Garfinkel, Rainwater, and Smeeding 2010; Gilbert 2010.
2. Adema and Ladaique 2009: Table 5.5; Fishback 2010: Table 5.
3. Howard 1997.
4. LIS 2010a.
5. Consumption tax rates are higher in the Nordic countries than in the United States. But these are incorporated in the purchasing power parities used to convert incomes to a common currency, so the income figures in third row of Table 9.1 are adjusted for differences in consumption taxes.
6. See also Figure 2.2.
7. Fishback 2010: 21.
8. OECD 2008: ch. 7.
9. See also Figure 4.1.
10. Currie 2006.
11. Esping-Andersen 1990: 21.

CHAPTER 10

1. Using the tenth-percentile-income-by-GDP-per-capita slopes from Figure 2.1 instead of the composite "progress for the poor" measure allows a focus on change over time (the material deprivation rates are for a single point in time) and inclusion of Canada and Switzerland. Doing so does not alter the conclusion suggested by the patterns in the charts in Figure 10.1.
2. Some of the indicators could serve for more than one outcome. For instance, political rights is an indicator of both liberty and capabilities. The share of 25-to-34-year-olds with at least an upper secondary education is an indicator of capabilities, opportunity, and social inclusion. And so on.
3. A similar pattern is found if instead of the level of per capita GDP I use the rate of per capita GDP growth over the period from 1979 to 2007, adjusted for "catching up" by initially poorer nations.
4. Its dominance, though, is increasingly questioned. See Stiglitz, Sen, and Fitoussi 2009.

5. The employment rate also serves as an indicator of reciprocity—the principle that all who are able to contribute do so. See Bowles and Gintis 1998; Galston 2001; Rawls 2001; White 2004.
6. Sen 1992, 1999; Robeyns 2005; Nussbaum 2006.
7. See Green 2006; Eurofound 2007; Gallie 2007; Antón et al. 2011.
8. The three social inclusion indicators I use are suggested in Atkinson et al. 2002, 2005.
9. The study of subjective well-being has proliferated. See for instance Layard 2005; Diener et al. 2009.
10. On the worry that generous social policies and/or other egalitarian institutions impede fiscal rectitude, see Iversen and Wren 1998; Scharpf 2000.
11. See, for example, Korpi 1985; Esping-Andersen 2004; Sjöberg 2010.

CHAPTER 11

1. Blank 1997*a*; Currie 2006; CAPTFP 2007; Haskins and Sawhill 2009.
2. See Castles et al. 2010.
3. Hicks 1999; Huber and Stephens 2001.
4. Gornick and Meyers 2003.
5. Immervoll and Pearson 2009.
6. Cohn 2010: 25.
7. Inglehart 1977; Inglehart and Abramson 1994.
8. McCall and Kenworthy 2009; Kenworthy 2010*b*.
9. Friedman 2005.
10. Meltzer and Richard 1981.
11. McCall and Kenworthy 2009.
12. Kenworthy and McCall 2008.
13. Hochschild 1981; Kluegal and Smith 1986; Gilens 1999; McCall and Kenworthy 2009; Page and Jacobs 2009; Kenworthy 2010*b*; McCall 2011.
14. Page and Jacobs 2009; Kenworthy 2010*b*.
15. Kenworthy 2010*b*.
16. Cohn 2010.
17. Page and Shapiro 1983; Shapiro and Young 1989; Burstein 1998; Alesina and Glaeser 2004; Brooks and Manza 2007; Howard 2007: ch. 6
18. Svallfors 1997, 2007; Rothstein 1998; Blekesaune and Quadagno 2003; Mettler and Soss 2004; Jaeger 2006; Larsen 2008; Kenworthy 2009*d*; Jordan 2010; Newman and Jacobs 2010.
19. Pierson 1994.
20. Pierson 2001; Castles 2004.
21. Hills, Sefton, and Stewart 2009; Smeeding and Waldfogel 2010; Waldfogel 2010.

22. Sefton, Hills, and Sutherland 2009: Figure 2.5.
23. Hills 2004: Table 8.3.
24. Amenta 1998; Moss 2002; Weaver 2009; Cohn 2010; Gitterman 2010.

References

Adema, Willem. 1997. "What Do Countries Really Spend on Social Policies? A Comparative Note." *OECD Economic Studies* 28: 153–67.

——2001. "Revisiting Real Social Spending Across Countries: A Brief Note." *OECD Economic Studies* 30: 191–7.

——Maxime Ladaique. 2009. "How Expensive is the Welfare State? Gross and Net Indicators in the OECD Social Expenditure Database (SOCX)." OECD Social, Employment, and Migration Working Paper 92. <oecd.org/els/workingpapers>.

Alber, Jens. 2010. "What the European and American Welfare States Have in Common and Where They Differ: Facts and Fiction in Comparisons of the European Social Model and the United States." *Journal of European Social Policy* 20: 102–25.

Alderson, Arthur S. and François Nielsen. 2002. "Globalization and the Great U-Turn: Income Inequality Trends in 16 OECD Countries." *American Journal of Sociology* 107: 1244–99.

Alesina, Alberto and Edward L. Glaeser. 2004. *Fighting Poverty in the US and Europe*. Oxford: Oxford University Press.

Alkire, Sabina and Maria Emma Santos. 2010. "Acute Multidimensional Poverty: A New Index for Developing Countries." Human Development Research Paper 2010-11. United Nations Development Programme. <hdr.undp.org/en/reports/global/hdr2010/papers/HDRP_2010_11.pdf>.

Amenta, Edwin. 1998. *Bold Relief: Institutional Politics and the Origins of Modern American Social Policy*. Princeton, NJ: Princeton University Press.

Andersson, Fredrik, Harry J. Holzer, and Julia I. Lane. 2005. *Moving Up or Moving On: Who Advances in the Low-Wage Labor Market*. New York: Russell Sage Foundation.

Andreß, Hans-Jürgen and Henning Lohmann, eds. 2008. *The Working Poor in Europe*. Cheltenham, UK: Edward Elgar.

Antón, José Ignacio, Rafael Muñoz de Bustillo, Enrique Fernández-Macías, and Fernando Esteve. 2011 (forthcoming). "E Pluribus Unum? A Critical Survey of Job Quality Indicators." *Socio-Economic Review*.

Arnold, Jens. 2008. "Do Tax Structures Affect Aggregate Economic Growth? Empirical Evidence from a Panel of OECD Countries." Economics Department Working Paper 643. Paris: OECD.

Atkinson, Anthony B. 1987. "On the Measurement of Poverty." *Econometrica* 55: 749–64.

Atkinson, Anthony B. 1999. *The Economic Consequences of Rolling Back the Welfare State*. Cambridge, MA: MIT Press.

——Andrea Brandolini. 2001. "Promise and Pitfalls in the Use of 'Secondary' Data-Sets: Income Inequality in OECD Countries as a Case Study." *Journal of Economic Literature* 39: 771–99.

——Bea Cantillon, Eric Marlier, and Brian Nolan. 2002. *Social Indicators: The EU and Social Inclusion*. Oxford: Oxford University Press.

————2005. *Taking Forward the EU Social Inclusion Process*. Report prepared for the Luxembourg Presidency of the Council of the European Union. <ceps.lu/actualites/details/event_28/attachments/final_-report.pdf>.

——Thomas Piketty, and Emmanuel Saez. 2009. "Top Incomes in the Long Run of History." Working Paper 15408. National Bureau of Economic Research. <nber.org>.

Bäckman, Olof. 2009. "Institutions, Structures, and Poverty: A Comparative Study of 16 Countries, 1980–2000." *European Sociological Review* 25: 251–24.

Bardone, Laura and Anne-Catherine Guio. 2005. "In-Work Poverty." Eurostat Statistics in Focus: Population and Living Conditions 5-2005.

Barro, Robert J. and Jong-Wha Lee. N.d. *International Data on Educational Attainment*. <cid.harvard.edu/ciddata/ciddata.html>.

Bartels, Larry. 1997. "Specification Uncertainty and Model Averaging." *American Journal of Political Science* 41: 641–74.

Barth, Erling and Karl Ove Moene. 2009. "The Equality Multiplier." Working Paper 15076. National Bureau of Economic Research. <nber.org>.

Baumol, William J., Alan S. Blinder, and Edward Wolff. 2003. *Downsizing in America*. New York: Russell Sage Foundation.

Bazen, Stephen, Mary Gregory, and Wiemer Salverda, eds. 1998. *Low-Wage Employment in Europe*. Northampton, MA: Edward Elgar.

Becker, Gary S. and Casey B. Mulligan. 2003. "Deadweight Costs and the Size of Government." *Journal of Law and Economics* 46: 293–340.

Behrendt, Christina. 2000. "Do Means-Tested Benefits Alleviate Poverty? Evidence on Germany, Sweden, and the United Kingdom from the Luxembourg Income Study." *Journal of European Social Policy* 10: 23–41.

Bentele, Keith Gunnar. 2009. *Rising Earnings Inequality in the United States: Determinants, Divergent Paths, and State Experiences*. Ph.D. dissertation. Department of Sociology. University of Arizona.

Beramendi, Pablo and David Rueda. 2007. "Social Democracy Constrained: Indirect Taxation in Industrialized Democracies." *British Journal of Political Science* 37: 619–41.

Bergh, Andreas. 2005. "On the Counterfactual Problem of Welfare State Research: How Can We Measure Redistribution?" *European Sociological Review* 21: 345–57.

——Martin Karlsson. 2010. "Government Size and Growth: Accounting for Economic Freedom and Globalization." *Public Choice* 142: 195–213.

Bernstein, Jared and Dean Baker. 2003. *The Benefits of Full Employment.* Washington, DC: Economic Policy Institute.

Beverly, Sondra G. 2001a. "Material Hardship in the United States: Evidence from the Survey of Income and Program Participation." *Social Work Research* 25: 143–51.

——2001b. "Measures of Material Hardship: Rationale and Recommendations." *Journal of Poverty* 5: 23–51.

Björklund, Anders and Richard Freeman. 2010. "Searching for Optimal Inequality/Incentives." Working Paper 14014. National Bureau of Economic Research. <nber.org>.

——Markus Jantti. 2009. "Intergenerational Income Mobility and the Role of Family Background." Pp. 491–521 in *The Oxford Handbook of Economic Inequality*, edited by Wiemer Salverda, Brian Nolan, and Timothy M. Smeeding. Oxford: Oxford University Press.

Blair, Tony. 2010. *A Journey: My Political Life.* New York: Knopf.

Blank, Rebecca M. 1997a. *It Takes a Nation: A New Agenda for Fighting Poverty.* New York and Princeton, NJ: Russell Sage Foundation and Princeton University Press.

——1997b. "Why Has Economic Growth Been Such an Ineffective Tool Against Poverty in Recent Years?" in *Poverty and Inequality: The Political Economy of Redistribution*, edited by Jon Neil. Kalamazoo. MI: Upjohn Institute for Employment Research.

——2000. "Fighting Poverty: Lessons from Recent U.S. History." *Journal of Economic Perspectives* 14: 3–19.

——2002. "Evaluating Welfare Reform in the United States." *Journal of Economic Literature* 40: 1105–66.

——2006. "Was Welfare Reform Successful?" *Economists Voice,* March. <bepress.com/ev>.

——2009. "Economic Change and the Structure of Opportunity for Less-Skilled Workers." Pp. 63–91 in *Changing Poverty, Changing Policies*, edited by Maria Cancian and Sheldon Danziger. New York: Russell Sage Foundation.

——Alan Blinder. 1986. "Macroeconomics, Income Distribution, and Poverty." Pp. 180–208 in *Fighting Poverty: What Works and What Doesn't*, edited by Sheldon Danziger and Daniel Weinberg. Cambridge, MA: Harvard University Press.

——David Card. 1993. "Poverty, Income Distribution, and Growth: Are They Still Connected?" *Brookings Papers on Economic Activity* 2: 285–339.

——Philip K. Robbins. 2000. "Financial Incentives for Increasing Work and Income among Low-Income Families." in *Finding Jobs: Work and Welfare*

Reform, edited by Rebecca M. Blank and David Card. New York: Russell Sage Foundation.

——Sheldon H. Danziger, and Robert F. Schoeni. 2006. "Work and Poverty During the Past Quarter-Century." Pp. 1–20 in *Working and Poor*, edited by Rebecca M. Blank, Sheldon H. Danziger, and Robert F. Schoeni. New York: Russell Sage Foundation.

Blau, Francine D. and Lawrence M. Kahn. 2002. *At Home and Abroad: U.S. Labor Market Performance in International Perspective*. New York: Russell Sage Foundation.

Blekesaune, Morten and Jill Quadagno. 2003. "Public Attitudes toward Welfare State Policies: A Comparative Analysis of 24 Nations." *European Sociological Review* 19: 415–27.

Boarini, Romina, Asa Johansson, and Marco Mira d'Ercole. 2006. "Alternative Measures of Well-Being." OECD Social, Employment, and Migration Working Paper 33. <oecd.org/els/workingpapers>.

——Marco Mira d'Ercole. 2006. "Measures of Material Deprivation in OECD Countries." OECD Social, Employment, and Migration Working Paper 37. <oecd.org/els/workingpapers>.

Bosch, Gerhard, Ken Mayhew, and Jérôme Gautié. 2010. "Industrial Relations, Legal Regulations, and Wage Setting." Pp. 91–146 in *Low-Wage Work in the Wealthy World*, edited by Jérôme Gautié and John Schmitt. New York: Russell Sage Foundation.

——Claudia Weinkopf, eds. 2008. *Low-Wage Work in Germany*. New York: Russell Sage Foundation.

Boushey, Heather, Chauna Brocht, Bethney Gundersen, and Jared Bernstein. 2001. *Hardships in America: The Real Story of Working Families*. Washington, DC: Economic Policy Institute.

Bowles, Samuel and Herbert Gintis. 1998. "Is Equality Passé? Homo Recriprocans and the Future of Egalitarian Politics." *Boston Review*, December–January.

Bradley, David, Evelyne Huber, Stephanie Moller, François Nielsen, and John Stephens. 2003. "Distribution and Redistribution in Postindustrial Democracies." *World Politics* 55: 193–228.

Bradshaw, Jonathan and Naomi Finch. 2003. "Overlaps in Dimensions of Poverty." *Journal of Social Policy* 32: 513–25.

Brady, David. 2009. *Rich Democracies, Poor People*. Oxford: Oxford University Press.

Brandolini, Andrea and Timothy M. Smeeding. 2006. "Inequality: International Evidence." In *The New Palgrave Dictionary of Economics*, edited by S.N. Durlauf and L.E. Blume. Basingstoke, UK: Palgrave Macmillan.

Brewer, Mike, Alastair Muriel, David Phillips, and Luke Sibieta. 2009. *Poverty and Inequality in the UK: 2009*. London: Institute for Fiscal Studies. <ifs.org.uk/publications/4524>.

Brooks, Clem and Jeff Manza. 2007. *Why Welfare States Persist: The Importance of Public Opinion in Democracies*. Chicago: University of Chicago Press.

Burchardt, Tania. 2000. "Social Exclusion: Concepts and Evidence." in *Breadline Europe: The Measurement of Poverty*, edited by David Gordon and Peter Townsend. Bristol: Policy Press.

Burkhauser, Richard V. 2009. "Deconstructing European Poverty Measures: What Relative and Absolute Scales Measure." *Journal of Policy Analysis and Management* 28: 715–25.

Burniaux, Jean-Marc, Flavio Padrini, and Nicola Brandt. 2006. "Labour Market Performance, Income Inequality, and Poverty in OECD Countries." Working Paper 500. Economics Department, OECD. <oecd.org>.

Burstein, Paul. 1998. "Bringing the Public Back In: Should Sociologists Consider the Impact of Public Opinion on Public Policy?" *Social Forces* 77: 27–62.

Callan, T., Brian Nolan, and Christopher Whelan. 1993. "Resources, Deprivation, and the Measurement of Poverty." *Journal of Social Policy* 22: 141–72.

Campbell, Andrea Louise. 2007. "Universalism, Targeting, and Participation." Pp. 121–40 in *Remaking America: Democracy and Public Policy in an Age of Inequality*, edited by Joe Soss, Jacob S. Hacker, and Suzanne Mettler. New York: Russell Sage Foundation.

Campbell, John L. and Ove K. Pedersen. 2007. "The Varieties of Capitalism and Hybrid Success: Denmark in the Global Economy." *Comparative Political Studies* 40: 307–32.

Cancian, Maria and Sheldon Danziger. 2009. "Changing Poverty and Changing Antipoverty Policies." Pp. 1–31 in *Changing Poverty, Changing Policies*, edited by Maria Cancian and Sheldon Danziger. New York: Russell Sage Foundation.

CAPTFP (Center for American Progress Task Force on Poverty). 2007. *From Poverty to Prosperity*. Washington, DC: Center for American Progress.

Castles, Francis G. 2004. *The Future of the Welfare State*. Oxford: Oxford University Press.

——2008. "What Welfare States Do: A Disaggregated Expenditure Approach." *Journal of Social Policy* 38: 45–62.

——Stephan Leibfried, Jane Lewis, Herbert Obinger, and Christopher Pierson, eds. 2010. *The Oxford Handbook of the Welfare State*. Oxford: Oxford University Press.

Chamberlain, Andrew and Gerald Prante. 2007. "Who Pays Taxes and Who Receives Government Spending?" Working Paper 1. Tax Foundation. <taxfoundation.org/publications/show/2282.html>.

Chen, Shaohua and Martin Ravallion. 2001. "How Did the World's Poorest Fare in the 1990s?" *Review of Income and Wealth* 47: 283–300.

Citro, Constance F. and Robert T. Michael, eds. 1995. *Measuring Poverty: A New Approach*. Washington, DC: National Academy Press.

Clayton, Richard and Jonas Pontusson. 1998. "Welfare-State Retrenchment Revisited: Entitlement Cuts, Public Sector Restructuring, and Inegalitarian Trends in Advanced Capitalist Societies." *World Politics* 51: 67–98.

Cohn, Jonathan. 2010. "How They Did It: The Inside Account of Health Care Reform's Triumph." *The New Republic*, 10 June: 14–25.

Collier, Paul. 2007. *The Bottom Billion*. Oxford: Oxford University Press.

Commission on Growth and Development. 2008. *The Growth Report*. Washington, DC: World Bank. <growthcommission.org>.

Cox, W. Michael and Richard Alm. 1999. *Myths of Rich and Poor*. New York: Basic Books.

Currie, Janet M. 2006. *The Invisible Safety Net*. Princeton, NJ: Princeton University Press.

Cusack, Thomas R. and Pablo Beramendi. 2006. "Taxing Work." *European Journal of Political Research* 45: 43–75.

DeFina, Robert H. 2002. "The Impact of Macroeconomic Performance on Alternative Poverty Measures." *Social Science Research* 31: 29–48.

——Kishor Thanawala. 2004. "International Evidence on the Impact of Transfers and Taxes on Alternative Poverty Indexes." *Social Science Research* 33: 322–38.

Dekkers, Gijs G.M. 2003. "Financial and Multidimensional Poverty in European Countries: Can the Former Be Used as a Proxy of the Latter?" IRISS Working Paper 2003-13. CEPS/INSTEAD. Differdange, Luxembourg. <ceps.lu/iriss>.

DeLong, J. Bradford. 2009. "Slow Income Growth and Absolute Poverty in the North Atlantic Region." Unpublished. <braddelong.posterous.com/slow-income-growth-and-absolute-poverty-in-th>.

de Neubourg Chris, Julie Castonguay, and Keetie Roelen. 2007. "Social Safety Nets and Targeted Social Assistance: Lessons from the European Experience." SP Discussion Paper 0718. Social Protection and Labor, The World Bank.

Diener, Ed, Richard E. Lucas, Ulrich Schimmack, and John F. Helliwell. 2009. *Well-Being for Public Policy*. Oxford: Oxford University Press.

Dollar, David and Aart Kraay. 2002. "Growth is Good for the Poor." *Journal of Economic Growth* 7: 195–225.

Duncan, Greg, Bjorn Gustafsson, Richard Hauser, Gunther Schmaus, Stephen Jenkins, Hans Messinger, Ruud Muffels, Brian Nolan, Jean-Claude Ray, and Wolfgang Voges. 1995. "Poverty and Social-Assistance Dynamics in the United States, Canada, and Europe." Pp. 67–108 in *Poverty, Inequality, and the Future of Social Policy*, edited by Katherine McFate, Roger Lawson, and William Julius Wilson. New York: Russell Sage Foundation.

Edin, Kathryn and Laura Lein. 1997. *Making Ends Meet: How Single Mothers Survive Welfare and Low-Wage Work*. New York: Russell Sage Foundation.

Edmark, Karin, Che-Yuan Liang, Eva Mörk, and Håkan Selin. 2010. "Evaluation of the Swedish Earned Income Tax Credit". Uppsala: Uppsala University.

Ehrenreich, Barbara. 2001. *Nickel and Dimed: On (Not) Getting By in America*. New York: Henry Holt and Company.

Ellwood, David. 2000. "Anti-Poverty Policy for Families in the Next Century." *Journal of Economic Perspectives* 14(1): 187–98.

Esping-Andersen, Gøsta. 1990. *The Three Worlds of Welfare Capitalism*. Princeton, NJ: Princeton University Press.

——1999. *Social Foundations of Postindustrial Economies*. Oxford: Oxford University Press.

——2004. "Unequal Opportunities and the Mechanisms of Social Inheritance." Pp. 289–314 in *Generational Income Mobility in North America and Europe*, edited by Miles Corak. Cambridge: Cambridge University Press.

——2009. *The Incomplete Revolution: Adapting to Women's New Roles*. Cambridge, UK: Polity.

——Duncan Gallie, Anton Hemerijck, and John Myles. 2002. *Why We Need a New Welfare State*. Oxford: Oxford University Press.

——John Myles. 2009. "Economic Inequality and the Welfare State." Pp. 639–64 in *The Oxford Handbook of Economic Inequality*, edited by Wiemer Salverda, Brian Nolan, and Timothy M. Smeeding. Oxford: Oxford University Press.

Eurofound (European Foundation for the Improvement of Living and Working Conditions). 2007. *Fourth European Working Conditions Survey*. <eurofound.europa.eu/publications/htmlfiles/ef0698.htm>.

——2009. "Trade Union Membership 2003–2008." <eurofound.europa.eu/docs/eiro/tn0904019s/tn0904019s.pdf>.

Firebaugh, Glenn and Frank D. Beck. 1994. "Does Economic Growth Benefit the Masses? Growth, Dependence, and Welfare in the Third World." *American Sociological Review* 59: 631–53.

Fishback, Price V. 2010. "Social Welfare Expenditures in the United States and the Nordic Countries: 1900–2003." Working Paper 15982. National Bureau of Economic Research. <nber.org>.

Fitzgerald, Joan. 2006. *Moving Up in the New Economy: Career Ladders for U.S. Workers*. Ithaca, NY: ILR Press.

Fölster, Stefan and Magnus Henrekson. 2001. "Growth Effects of Government Expenditure and Taxation in Rich Countries." *European Economic Review* 45: 1501–20.

Förster, Michael and Marco Mira d'Ercole. 2005. "Income Distribution and Poverty in OECD Countries in the Second Half of the 1990s." OECD Social, Employment, and Migration Working Paper 22. <oecd.org/els/workingpapers>.

——Mark Pearson. 2002. "Income Distribution and Poverty in the OECD Area: Trends and Driving Forces." *OECD Economic Studies* 34: 7–39.

Freedom House. 2007. "Freedom in the World 2007 Subscores." <freedom house.org/template.cfm?page=372&year=2007>.

Freeman, Richard B. 2001. "The Rising Tide Lifts . . .?" Pp. 97–126 in *Understanding Poverty*, edited by Sheldon Danziger and Robert Haveman. New York and Cambridge, MA: Russell Sage Foundation and Harvard University Press.

——William M. Rodgers III. 2005. "The Weak Jobs Recovery: Whatever Happened to 'the Great American Jobs Machine'?" Federal Reserve Bank of New York *Economic Policy Review*, August: 3–18.

Friedman, Benjamin M. 2005. *The Moral Consequences of Economic Growth*. New York: Knopf.

Friedman, Milton. 1962. *Capitalism and Freedom*. Chicago: University of Chicago Press.

——Rose Friedman. 1979. *Free to Choose*. San Diego: Harcourt Brace Jovanovich.

Frohlich, Norman, Joe A. Oppenheimer, and Cheryl L. Eavey. 1987. "Laboratory Results on Rawls's Distributive Justice." *British Journal of Political Science* 17: 1–21.

Gallie, Duncan. 2002. "The Quality of Working Life in Welfare Strategy." Pp. 96–129 in *Why We Need a New Welfare State*, edited by Gøsta Esping-Andersen et al. Oxford: Oxford University Press.

——2003. "The Quality of Working Life: Is Scandinavia Different?" *European Sociological Review* 19: 61–79.

——, ed. 2007. *Employment Regimes and the Quality of Work*. Oxford: Oxford University Press.

Galston, William A. 2001. "What about Reciprocity?" Pp. 29–33 in *What's Wrong with a Free Lunch?* edited by Joshua Cohen and Joel Rogers. Boston: Beacon Press.

Ganghof, Steffen. 2000. "Adjusting National Tax Policy to Economic Internationalization: Strategies and Outcomes." Pp. 597–645 in *Welfare and Work in the Open Economy. Volume II: Diverse Responses to Common Challenges*, edited by Fritz W. Scharpf and Vivien A. Schmidt. Oxford: Oxford University Press.

——2005. "Globalization, Tax Reform Ideals, and Social Policy Financing." *Global Social Policy* 5: 77–95.

——2006. "Tax Mixes and the Size of the Welfare State: Causal Mechanisms and Policy Implications." *Journal of European Social Policy* 16: 360–73.

——2007. "The Political Economy of High Income Taxation: Capital Taxation, Path Dependence, and Political Institutions in Denmark." *Comparative Political Studies* 40: 1059–84.

Garfinkel, Irwin, Lee Rainwater, and Timothy Smeeding. 2010. *Wealth and Welfare States*. Oxford: Oxford University Press.

Gautié, Jérôme and John Schmitt, eds. 2010. *Low-Wage Work in the Wealthy World*. New York: Russell Sage Foundation.

Gelbach, Jonah B. and Lant H. Pritchett. 1995. "Does More for the Poor Mean Less for the Poor?" Working Paper 1523. Policy Research Department, Poverty and Human Resources Division, The World Bank.

Genschel, Philipp. 2002. "Globalization, Tax Competition, and the Welfare State." *Politics and Society* 30: 245–75.

Gießelmann, Marco and Henning Lohmann. 2008. "The Different Roles of Low-Wage Work in Germany: Regional, Demographical, and Temporal Variances in the Poverty Risk of Low-Paid Workers." Pp. 96–123 in *The Working Poor in Europe*, edited by Hans-Jürgen Andreß and Henning Lohmann. Cheltenham, UK: Edward Elgar.

Gilbert, Neil. 2002. *Transformation of the Welfare State: The Silent Surrender of Public Responsibility*. Oxford: Oxford University Press.

——2010. "Comparative Analyses of Stateness and State Action: What Can We Learn from Patterns of Expenditure?" Pp. 133–50 in *United in Diversity? Comparing Social Models in Europe and America*, edited by Jens Alber and Neil Gilbert. Oxford: Oxford University Press.

Gilens, Martin. 1999. *Why Americans Hate Welfare*. Chicago: University of Chicago Press.

Gitterman, Daniel P. 2010. *Boosting Paychecks: The Politics of Supporting America's Working Poor*. Washington, DC: Brookings Institution Press.

Goldin, Claudia and Lawrence F. Katz. 2008. *The Race between Education and Techology*. Cambridge, MA: Harvard University Press.

Goodin, Robert E., Bruce Headey, Ruud Muffels, and Henk-Jan Dirven. 1999. *The Real Worlds of Welfare Capitalism*. Cambridge: Cambridge University Press.

Gordon, David, Ruth Levitas, Christina Pantazis, Demi Patsios, Sarah Payne, Peter Townsend, Laura Adelman, Karl Ashworth, Sue Middleton, Jonathan Bradshaw, and Julie Williams. 2000. *Poverty and Social Exclusion in Britain*. York: Joseph Rowntree Foundation.

——Christina Pantazis, eds. 1997. *Breadline Britain in the 1990s*. Aldershot, UK: Ashgate.

Gornick, Janet C. and Marcia K. Meyers. 2003. *Families That Work: Policies for Reconciling Parenthood and Employment*. New York: Russell Sage Foundation.

Green, Francis. 2006. *Demanding Work: The Paradox of Job Quality in the Affluent Economy*. Princeton, NJ: Princeton University Press.

Greenstein, Robert. 1991. "Universal and Targeted Approaches to Relieving Poverty: An Alternative View." Pp. 437–59 in *The Urban Underclass*, edited by Christopher Jencks and Paul E. Peterson. Washington, DC: Brookings Institution.

Gregory, Mary, Wiemer Salverda, and Stephen Bazen, eds. 2000. *Labour Market Inequalities*. Oxford: Oxford University Press.

Griffin, Larry J., Pamela Barnhouse Walters, Phillip O'Connell, and Edward Moor. 1986. "Methodological Innovations in the Analysis of Welfare-State Development: Pooling Cross Sections and Time Series." Pp. 101–38 in *Futures for the Welfare State*, edited by Norman Furniss. Bloomington: Indiana University Press.

Gundersen, Craig and James P. Ziliak. 2004. "Poverty and Macroeconomic Performance Across Space, Race, and Family Structure." *Demography* 41: 61–86.

Hacker, Jacob S. 2002. *The Divided Welfare State*. Cambridge: Cambridge University Press.

Hall, Peter A. and Daniel W. Gingerich. 2004. "Varieties of Capitalism and Institutional Complementarities in the Macroeconomy: An Empirical Analysis." Discussion Paper 04/5. Max Planck Institute for the Study of Societies. Cologne, Germany. <mpi-fg-koeln.mpg.de>.

——David Soskice. 2001. "An Introduction to Varieties of Capitalism." Pp. 1–68 in *Varieties of Capitalism*, edited by Peter A. Hall and David Soskice. Oxford: Oxford University Press.

Halleröd, Björn. 1995. "The Truly Poor: Direct and Indirect Consensual Measurement of Poverty in Sweden." *Journal of European Social Policy* 5: 111–29.

——1996. "Deprivation and Poverty: A Comparative Analysis of Sweden and Great Britain." *Acta Sociologica* 39: 141–68.

——Daniel Larsson. 2008. "In-Work Poverty in a Transitional Labour Market: Sweden, 1988–2003." Pp. 155–78 in *The Working Poor in Europe*, edited by Hans-Jürgen Andreß and Henning Lohmann. Cheltenham, UK: Edward Elgar.

Halvorsen, Knut and Steinar Stjernø. 2008. *Work, Oil, and Welfare: The Welfare State in Norway*. Universitetsforlaget.

Haskins, Ron and Isabel Sawhill. 2009. *Creating an Opportunity Society*. Washington, DC: Brookings Institution Press.

Haveman, Robert and Jonathan Schwabish. 2000. "Has Macroeconomic Performance Regained Its Antipoverty Bite?" *Contemporary Economic Policy* 18: 415–27.

——Edward Wolff. 2005. "The Concept and Measurement of Asset Poverty: Levels, Trends, and Composition for the U.S., 1983–2001." *Journal of Economic Inequality* 2: 145–69.

Hemerijck, Anton. 2012 (forthcoming). *Changing Welfare States*. Oxford: Oxford University Press.

——Werner Eichhorst. 2009. "Whatever Happened to the Bismarckian Welfare State? From Labor Shedding to Employment-Friendly Reforms." IZA Discussion Paper 4085. <iza.org>.

Herzenberg, Stephen A., John A. Alic, and Howard Wial. 1998. *New Rules for a New Economy*. A Century Fund Book. Ithaca, NY: ILR Press.

Hicks, Alexander. 1999. *Social Democracy and Welfare Capitalism*. Ithaca, NY: Cornell University Press.

Hills, John. 2004. *Inequality and the State*. Oxford: Oxford University Press.

——Tom Sefton, and Kitty Stewart, eds. 2009. *Towards a More Equal Society? Poverty, Inequality, and Policy since 1997*. Bristol, U.K.: Policy Press.

Hochschild, Jennifer. 1981. *What's Fair? American Beliefs about Distributive Justice*. Cambridge, MA: Harvard University Press.

Hoffman, Saul D. and Laurence S. Seidman. 2003. *Helping Working Families: The Earned Income Tax Credit*. Kalamazoo, MI: Upjohn Institute for Employment Research.

Hotz, V. Joseph and John Karl Scholz. 2004. "The Earned Income Tax Credit." Pp. 141–97 in *Means-Tested Transfer Programs in the United States*, edited by Robert Moffitt. Chicago: University of Chicago Press.

Howard, Christopher. 1997. *The Hidden Welfare State*. Princeton, NJ: Princeton University Press.

——2007. *The Welfare State Nobody Knows*. Princeton, NJ: Princeton University Press.

Howell, David R., ed. 2005. *Fighting Unemployment: The Limits of Free Market Orthodoxy*. Oxford: Oxford University Press.

Hoxby, Caroline. 2003. "Our Favorite Method of Redistribution: School Spending Equality, Income Inequality, and Growth." Unpublished. Department of Economics, Harvard University.

Hoynes, Hilary W., Marianne E. Page, and Ann Huff Stevens. 2006. "Poverty in America: Trends and Explanations." *Journal of Economic Perspectives* 20(1): 47–68.

Huber, Evelyne and John D. Stephens. 2001. *Development and Crisis of the Welfare State*. Chicago: University of Chicago Press.

Huo, Jingjing, Moira Nelson, and John Stephens. 2008. "Decommodification and Activation in Social Democratic Policy: Resolving the Paradox." *Journal of European Social Policy* 18: 5–20.

Iceland, John. 2003. *Poverty in America*. Berkeley: University of California Press.

——Kurt Bauman. 2007. "Income Poverty and Material Hardship." *Journal of Socio-Economics* 36: 376–96.

——Lane Kenworthy, and Melissa Scopilliti. 2005. "Macroeconomic Performance and Poverty in the 1980s and 1990s: A State-Level Analysis."

Discussion Paper 1299-05. Institute for Research on Poverty, University of Wisconsin. <irp.wisc.edu/publications/dps/pdfs/dp129905.pdf>.

Immervoll, Herwig and Mark Pearson. 2009. "A Good Time for Making Work Pay? Taking Stock of In-Work Benefits and Related Measures Across the OECD." *OECD Social, Employment, and Migration Working Paper* 81. <oecd.org/els/workingpapers>.

Inglehart, Ronald. 1977. *The Silent Revolution: Changing Values and Political Styles among Western Publics.* Princeton, NJ: Princeton University Press.

——Paul R. Abramson. 1994. "Economic Security and Value Change." *American Political Science Review* 88: 336–54.

Iversen, Torben and Anne Wren. 1998. "Equality, Employment, and Budgetary Restraint: The Trilemma of the Service Economy." *World Politics* 50: 507–46.

Jackman, Robert W. 1985. "Cross-National Statistical Research and the Study of Politics." *American Journal of Political Science* 29: 161–82.

Jaeger, Mads Meier. 2006. "Welfare Regimes and Attitudes Towards Redistribution: The Welfare Regime Hypothesis Revisited." *European Sociological Review* 22: 157–70.

Jencks, Christopher. 1992. *Rethinking Social Policy.* Cambridge, MA: Harvard University Press.

——2005. "What Happened to Welfare?" *New York Review of Books,* 15 December: 76–81, 86.

Jonsson, Jan, Carina Mood, and Erik Bihagen. 2010. "Poverty in Sweden 1991–2007." Swedish Institute for Social Research, Stockholm University.

Jordan, Jason. 2010. "Institutional Feedback and Support for the Welfare State: The Case of National Health Care." *Comparative Political Studies* 43: 862–85.

Kangas, Olli. 2000. "Distributive Justice and Social Policy: Some Reflections on Rawls and Income Distribution." *Social Policy and Administration* 34: 520–8.

——2002. "Economic Growth, Inequality, and the Economic Position of the Poor in 1985–1995: An International Perspective." *International Journal of Health Services* 32: 213–27.

——Joakim Palme. 2000. "Does Social Policy Matter? Poverty Cycles in OECD Countries." *International Journal of Health Services* 30: 335–52.

Kato, Junko. 2003. *Regressive Taxation and the Welfare State.* Cambridge: Cambridge University Press.

Kemmerling, Achim. 2005. "Tax Mixes, Welfare States, and Employment: Tracking Diverging Vulnerabilities." *Journal of European Public Policy* 12: 1–22.

——2009. *Taxing the Working Poor.* London: Edward Elgar.

Kenworthy, Lane. 1995. *In Search of National Economic Success: Balancing Competition and Cooperation.* Thousand Oaks, CA: Sage.

——1999. "Do Social-Welfare Policies Reduce Poverty? A Cross-National Assessment." *Social Forces* 77: 1119–39.

——2004. *Egalitarian Capitalism*. New York: Russell Sage Foundation.

——2006. "Institutional Coherence and Macroeconomic Performance." *Socio-Economic Review* 4: 69–91.

——2007. "Toward Improved Use of Regression in Macrocomparative Analysis." *Comparative Social Research* 24: 343–50.

——2008a. "Has Ireland's Rising Tide Benefited Its Poor?" *Consider the Evidence*. <considertheevidence.net/2008/05/18/has-irelands-rising-tide-benefited-its-poor>.

——2008b. *Jobs with Equality*. Oxford: Oxford University Press.

——2009a. "How Progressive Are Our Taxes?" *Consider the Evidence*. <considertheevidence.net/2009/01/05/how-progressive-are-our-taxes>.

——2009b. "How Progressive Are Our Taxes? Follow-Up." *Consider the Evidence*. <considertheevidence.net/2009/01/08/how-progressive-are-our-taxes-follow-up>.

——2009c. "Reducing Inequality: Are Unions the Answer?" *Crooked Timber*. <crookedtimber.org/2009/04/14/reducing-inequality-are-unions-the-answer>.

——2009d. "The Effect of Public Opinion on Social Policy Generosity." *Socio-Economic Review* 7: 727–40.

——2009e. "The High-Employment Route to Low Inequality." *Challenge* 52 (5): 77–99.

——2010a. "Rising Inequality, Public Policy, and America's Poor." *Challenge* 53(6): 93–109.

——2010b. "What Do Americans Want?" <u.arizona.edu/~lkenwor/lecture-whatdoamericanswant.pdf>.

——Leslie McCall. 2008. "Inequality, Public Opinion, and Redistribution." *Socio-Economic Review* 6: 35–68.

——Jonas Pontusson. 2005. "Rising Inequality and the Politics of Redistribution in Affluent Countries." *Perspectives on Politics* 3: 449–71.

Kim, Hwanjoon. 2000. "Anti-Poverty Effectiveness of Taxes and Income Transfers in Welfare States." *International Social Security Review* 53(4): 105–29.

King, Miriam, Steven Ruggles, Trent Alexander, Donna Leicach, and Matthew Sobek. 2004. *Integrated Public Use Microdata Series: Current Population Survey, Version 2.0*. Machine-readable database. Produced and distributed by the Minnesota Population Center. <cps.ipums.org/cps>.

Kittel, Bernhard. 1999. "Sense and Sensitivity in Pooled Analysis of Political Data." *European Journal of Political Research* 35: 225–53.

Kluegal, James R. and Eliot R. Smith. 1986. *Beliefs about Inequality*. New York: Aldine De Gruyter.

Korpi, Walter. 1980. "Approaches to the Study of Poverty in the United States: Critical Notes from a European Perspective." Pp. 287–314 in *Poverty and Public Policy*, edited by V.T. Covello. Boston: Schenkman.

——1985. "Economic Growth and the Welfare State: Leaky Bucket or Irrigation System?" *European Sociological Review* 1: 97–118.

——Joakim Palme. 1998. "The Paradox of Redistribution and Strategies of Equality: Welfare State Institutions, Inequality, and Poverty in the Western Countries." *American Sociological Review* 63: 661–87.

Kozol, Jonathan. 1991. *Savage Inequalities: Children in America's Schools.* New York: Crown.

Krugman, Paul. 1996. "The Causes of High Unemployment." *Policy Options*, July–August: 20–4.

Kuznets, Simon. 1955. "Economic Growth and Income Inequality." *American Economic Review* 45: 1–28.

Larsen, Christian Albrekt. 2008. "The Institutional Logic of Welfare Attitudes: How Welfare Regimes Influence Public Support." *Comparative Political Studies* 41: 145–68.

Layard, Richard. 2005. *Happiness: Lessons from a New Science.* New York: Penguin.

Layte, Richard, Bertrand Maître, Brian Nolan, and Christopher T. Whelan. 2001. "Persistent and Consistent Poverty in the 1994 and 1995 Waves of the European Community Household Panel Survey." *Review of Income and Wealth* 47: 427–49.

——Brian Nolan, and Christopher T. Whelan. 2000. "Targeting Poverty: Lessons from Monitoring Ireland's National Anti-Poverty Strategy." *Journal of Social Policy* 29: 553–75.

——Christopher T. Whelan, Bertrand Maître, and Brian Nolan. 2001. "Explaining Levels of Deprivation in the European Union." *Acta Sociologica* 44: 105–21.

Leamer, Edward E. 1983. "Let's Take the Con out of Econometrics." *American Economic Review* 73: 31–43.

——1985. "Sensitivity Analyses Would Help." *American Economic Review* 75: 308–13.

Lebergott, Stanley. 1976. *The American Economy.* Princeton, NJ: Princeton University Press.

Lindert, Peter. 2004. *Growing Public: Social Spending and Economic Growth since the Eighteenth Century.* Two volumes. Cambridge: Cambridge University Press.

LIS (Luxembourg Income Study). 2010a. "LIS Database." <lisproject.org/techdoc.htm>.

——2010b. "LIS Key Figures." <lisproject.org/key-figures/key-figures.htm>.

Lohmann, Henning. 2008. "The Working Poor in European Welfare States: Empirical Evidence from a Multilevel Perspective." Pp. 47–74 in *The*

Working Poor in Europe, edited by Hans-Jürgen Andreß and Henning Lohmann. Cheltenham, UK: Edward Elgar.

——Hans-Jürgen Andreß. 2008. "Explaining In-Work Poverty within and across Countries." Pp. 293–313 in *The Working Poor in Europe*, edited by Hans-Jürgen Andreß and Henning Lohmann. Cheltenham, UK: Edward Elgar.

——Ive Marx. 2008. "The Different Faces of In-Work Poverty across Welfare State Regimes." Pp. 17–46 in *The Working Poor in Europe*, edited by Hans-Jürgen Andreß and Henning Lohmann. Cheltenham, UK: Edward Elgar.

Lucifora, Claudio, Abigail McKnight, and Wiemer Salverda. 2005. "Low-Wage Employment in Europe: A Review of the Evidence." *Socio-Economic Review* 3: 259–92.

Mack, J. and S. Lansley. 1985. *Poor Britain.* London: George Allen and Unwin.

Mahler, Vincent and David Jesuit. 2006. "Fiscal Redistribution in the Developed Countries: New Insights from the Luxembourg Income Study." *Socio-Economic Review* 4: 483–511.

Marical, François, Marco Mira d'Ercole, Maria Vaalavuo, and Gerlinde Verbist. 2006. "Publicly-Provided Services and the Distribution of Resources." OECD Social, Employment, and Migration Working Paper 45. <oecd.org/els/workingpapers>.

Marlier, Eric, Bea Cantillon, Brian Nolan, and K. Van den Bosch. 2009. "Developing and Learning from Measures of Social Inclusion in the European Union." OECD conference on Measuring Poverty, Income Inequality, and Social Exclusion, Paris, March.

Marx, Ive and Gerlinde Verbist. 1998. "Low-Paid Work and Poverty: A Cross-Country Perspective." Pp. 63–86 in *Low-Wage Employment in Europe*, edited by Stephan Bazen, Mary Gregory, and Wiemer Salverda. Cheltenham, MA: Edward Elgar.

——2008a. "Combating In-Work Poverty in Europe: The Policy Options Assessed." Pp. 273–92 in *The Working Poor in Europe*, edited by Hans-Jürgen Andreß and Henning Lohmann. Cheltenham, UK: Edward Elgar.

——2008b. "When Famialism Fails: The Nature and Causes of In-Work Poverty in Belgium." Pp. 77–95 in *The Working Poor in Europe*, edited by Hans-Jürgen Andreß and Henning Lohmann. Cheltenham, UK: Edward Elgar.

Matsaganis, M. et al. 2004. "Child Poverty and Family Transfers in Southern Europe." Euromod Working Paper EM2-04.

Mayer, Susan E. 1993. "Living Conditions Among the Poor in Four Rich Countries." *Journal of Population Economics* 6: 261–86.

——1995. "A Comparison of Poverty and Living Conditions in the United States, Canada, Sweden, and Germany." Pp. 109–51 in *Poverty, Inequality, and the Future of Social Policy*, edited by Katherine McFate, Roger Lawson, and William Julius Wilson. New York: Russell Sage Foundation.

——Christopher Jencks. 1989. "Poverty and the Distribution of Material Hardship." *Journal of Human Resources* 24: 88–114.

McCall, Leslie. 2011. *The Undeserving Rich*. Unpublished. Northwestern University.

——Lane Kenworthy. 2009. "Americans' Social Policy Prefeences in the Era of Rising Inequality." *Perspectives on Politics* 7: 459–84.

Medrano, Jaime Díez. 2010. "Interpersonal Trust." <jdsurvey.net/jds/jdsurveyMaps.jsp?Idioma=I&SeccionTexto=0404&NOID=104>.

Meltzer, Allan H. and Scott F. Richard. 1981. "A Rational Theory of the Size of Government." *Journal of Political Economy* 89: 914–27.

Mettler, Suzanne and Joe Soss. 2004. "The Consequences of Public Policy for Democratic Citizenship: Bridging Policy Studies and Mass Publics." *Perspectives on Politics* 2: 55–73.

Meyer, Bruce D. and James X. Sullivan. 2009. "Five Decades of Consumption and Income Poverty." Working Paper 14827. National Bureau of Economic Research. <nber.org>.

Meyer, Daniel R. and Geoffrey L. Wallace. 2009. "Poverty Levels and Trends in Comparative Perspective." Pp. 35–62 in *Changing Poverty, Changing Policies*, edited by Maria Cancian and Sheldon Danziger. New York: Russell Sage Foundation.

Mishel, Lawrence, Jared Bernstein, and Heidi Shierholz. 2009. *The State of Working America, 2008/2009*. An Economic Policy Institute Book. Ithaca, NY: ILR Press.

Mitchell, Deborah. 1991. *Income Transfers in Ten Welfare States*. Brookfield: Avebury.

Moene, Karl Ove and Michael Wallerstein. 2001. "Targeting and Political Support for Welfare Spending." *Economics of Governance* 2: 3–24.

Moffitt, Robert and John Karl Scholz. 2009. "Trends in the Level and Distribution of Income Support." Working Paper 15488. National Bureau of Economic Research. <nber.org>.

Moller, Stephanie, David Bradley, Evelyne Huber, François Nielsen, and John D. Stephens. 2003. "Determinants of Relative Poverty in Advanced Capitalist Democracies." *American Sociological Review* 68: 22–51.

Moss, David A. 2002. *When All Else Fails: Government as the Ultimate Risk Manager*. Cambridge, MA: Harvard University Press.

Muffels, Ruud and Didier Fourage. 2004. "The Role of European Welfare States in Explaining Resources Deprivation." *Social Indicators Research* 68: 299–330.

Murray, Charles. 1984. *Losing Ground: American Social Policy, 1950–1980*. New York: Basic Books.

Myles, Gareth D. 2009. "Economic Growth and the Role of Taxation: Aggregate Data." OECD Economics Department Working Paper 714. <olis.oecd.org/olis/2009doc.nsf/linkto/eco-wkp(2009)55>.

Myles, John, Feng Hou, Garnett Picot, and Karen Myers. 2009. "The Demographic Foundations of Rising Employment and Earnings among Single Mothers in Canada and the United States, 1980–2000." *Population Research and Policy Review.*

Nelson, Kenneth. 2004. "The Formation of Minimum Income Protection." Working Paper 373. Luxembourg Income Study. <lisproject.org>.

——2007. "Universalism versus Targeting: The Vulnerability of Social Insurance and Means-Tested Minimum Income Protection in 18 Countries, 1990–2002." *International Social Security Review* 60: 33–58.

Newman, Katherine S. and Elizabeth S. Jacobs. 2010. *Who Cares? Public Ambivalence and Government Activism from the New Deal to the Second Gilded Age.* Princeton, NJ: Princeton University Press.

Nolan, Brian. 2008. "Low Pay and Household Poverty during Ireland's Economic Boom." Pp. 250–70 in *The Working Poor in Europe*, edited by Hans-Jürgen Andreß and Henning Lohmann. Cheltenham, UK: Edward Elgar.

——Ive Marx. 2000. "Low Pay and Household Poverty." Pp. 100–19 in *Labour Market Inequalities*, edited by Mary Gregory, Wiemer Salverda, and Stephen Bazen. Oxford: Oxford University Press.

——2009. "Economic Inequality, Poverty, and Social Exclusion." Pp. 315–41 in *The Oxford Handbook of Economic Inequality*, edited by Wiemer Salverda, Brian Nolan, and Timothy M. Smeeding. Oxford: Oxford University Press.

——Christopher T. Whelan. 1996. *Resources, Deprivation, and Poverty.* Oxford: Clarendon Press.

——2010. "Using Non-Monetary Deprivation Indicators to Analyze Poverty and Social Exclusion: Lessons from Europe?" *Journal of Policy Analysis and Management* 29: 305–25.

Nussbaum, Martha. 2006. "Poverty and Human Functioning: Capabilities as Fundamental Entitlements." Pp. 47–75 in *Poverty and Inequality*, edited by David Grusky and Ravi Kanbar. Stanford, CA: Stanford University Press.

OECD (Organization for Economic Cooperation and Development). 1994. *The OECD Jobs Study.* Paris: OECD.

——2001. "When Money is Tight: Poverty Dynamics in OECD Countries." Pp. 37–87 in *OECD Employment Outlook.* Paris: OECD.

——2005. *Extending Opportunities: How Active Social Policy Can Benefit Us All.* Paris: OECD.

——2006. *OECD Employment Outlook: Boosting Jobs and Incomes.* Paris: OECD.

148   *References*

OECD (Organization for Economic Cooperation and Development). 2007. "Financing Social Protection: The Employment Effect." Pp. 157–206 in *OECD Employment Outlook*. Paris: OECD.

——2008. *Growing Unequal?* Paris: OECD.

——2009a. *Education at a Glance*. Paris: OECD.

——2009b. "Is Work the Best Antidote to Poverty?" Pp. 165–210 in *OECD Employment Outlook*. Paris: OECD.

——2010. *OECD.Stat*. Online database. <sourceoecd.org/database/ OECDStat>.

Okun, Arthur M. 1975. *Equality and Efficiency: The Big Tradeoff*. Washington, DC: Brookings Institution.

Osberg, Lars and K. Xu. 2000. "International Comparisons of Poverty Intensity: Index Decomposition and Bootstrap Inference." *Journal of Human Resources* 35: 51–81.

Page, Benjamin and Lawrence Jacobs. 2009. *Class War? What Americans Really Think about Economic Inequality*. Chicago: University of Chicago Press.

——Robert Y. Shapiro. 1983. "Effects of Public Opinion on Policy." *American Political Science Review* 77: 175–90.

Palier, Bruno. 2000. "'Defrosting' the French Welfare State." *West European Politics* 23: 113–36.

——Claude Martin. 2007. "From 'a Frozen Landscape' to Structural Reforms: The Sequential Transformation of Bismarckian Welfare Systems." *Social Policy and Administration* 41: 535–54.

Palme, Joakim. 2006. "Welfare States and Inequality: Institutional Designs and Distributive Outcome." *Research in Social Stratification and Mobility* 24: 387–403.

——Åke Bergmark, Olof Bäckman, Felipe Estrada, Johan Fritzell, Olle Lundberg, Ola Sjöberg, Lena Sommestad, and Marta Szebehely. 2002. *Welfare in Sweden: The Balance Sheet for the 1990s*. Stockholm: Ministry of Health and Social Affairs.

Paulus, Alari, Holly Sutherland, and Panos Tsakloglou. 2010. "The Distributional Impact of In-Kind Public Benefits in European Countries." *Journal of Policy Analysis and Management* 29: 243–66.

Perry, Bryan. 2002. "The Mismatch between Income Measures and Direct Outcome Measures of Poverty." *Social Policy Journal of New Zealand* 19: 101–27.

Picot, G., R. Morissette, and John Myles. 2003. "Low-Income Intensity During the 1990s: The Role of Economic Growth, Employment Earnings, and Social Transfers." *Canadian Public Policy* 29: S15–S40.

Pierson, Paul. 1994. *Dismantling the Welfare State? Reagan, Thatcher, and the Politics of Retrenchment*. Cambridge: Cambridge University Press.

——2001a. "Coping with Permanent Austerity: Welfare State Restructuring in Affluent Democracies." Pp. 410–56 in *The New Politics of the Welfare State*, edited by Paul Pierson. Oxford: Oxford University Press.

——, ed. 2001b. *The New Politics of the Welfare State*. Oxford: Oxford University Press.

Pontusson, Jonas. 2005. *Inequality and Prosperity*. Ithaca, NY: Cornell University Press.

——2011 (forthcoming). "Once Again a Model: Nordic Social Democracy in a Globalized World." in *Futures of the Left*, edited by James Cronin, George Ross, and James Shoch. Durham, NC: Duke University Press.

Prasad, Monica and Yingying Deng. 2009. "Taxation and the Worlds of Welfare." *Socio-Economic Review* 7: 431–57.

Rainwater, Lee. 1982. "Stigma in Income-Tested Programs." Pp. 19–46 in *Income-Tested Transfer Programs*, edited by Irwin Garfinkel. New York: Academic Press.

——Timothy M. Smeeding. 2003. *Poor Kids in a Rich Country*. New York: Russell Sage Foundation.

Rawls, John. 1971. *A Theory of Justice*. Cambridge, MA: Harvard University Press.

——2001. *Justice as Fairness: A Restatement*, edited by Erin Kelly. Cambridge, MA: Harvard University Press.

Reber, Sarah and Laura Tyson. 2004. "Rising Health Insurance Costs Slow Job Growth and Reduce Wages and Job Quality." Unpublished. Kaiser Family Foundation.

Rector, Robert E., Kirk A. Johnson, and Sarah E. Youssef. 1999. "The Extent of Material Hardship and Poverty in the United States." *Review of Social Economy* 57: 351–87.

——2004. *Understanding Poverty in America*. Backgrounder 1713. Washington, DC: Heritage Foundation.

Ringen, Stein. 1987. *The Possibility of Politics: A Study in the Political Economy of the Welfare State*. Oxford: Clarendon Press.

——1988. "Direct and Indirect Measures of Poverty." *Journal of Social Policy* 17: 351–65.

Robeyns, Ingrid. 2005. "The Capability Approach: A Theoretical Survey." *Journal of Human Development* 6: 93–114.

Rodrik, Dani. 2007. *One Economics, Many Recipes*. Princeton, NJ: Princeton University Press.

Rothstein, Bo. 1998. *Just Institutions Matter: The Moral and Political Logic of the Universal Welfare State*. Cambridge: Cambridge University Press.

——2010 (forthcoming). "Corruption, Happiness, Social Trust, and the Welfare State." *Social Research*.

Rueda, David. 2007. *Social Democracy Inside Out*. Oxford: Oxford University Press.

Saunders, Peter. 2010. "Inequality and Poverty." Pp. 526–38 in *The Oxford Handbook of the Welfare State*, edited by Francis G. Castles, Stephan

Leibfried, Jane Lewis, Herbert Obinger, and Christopher Pierson. Oxford: Oxford University Press.

——Laura Adelman. 2005. "Income Poverty, Deprivation, and Exclusion: A Comparative Study of Australia and Britain." Discussion Paper 141. Social Policy Research Centre. University of New South Wales.

——Bruce Bradbury. 2006. "Monitoring Trends in Poverty and Income Distribution: Data, Methodology, and Measurement." *Economic Record* 82: 341–64.

Sawhill, Isabell. 1988. "Poverty in the U.S.: Why Is It So Persistent?" *Journal of Economic Literature* 26: 1073–119.

Scharpf, Fritz W. 1997. "Employment and the Welfare State: A Continental Dilemma." Working Paper 97/7. Max Planck Institute for the Study of Societies. <mpifg.de>.

——2000. "The Viability of Advanced Welfare States in the International Economy: Vulnerabilities and Options." *Journal of European Public Policy* 7: 190–228.

——Vivien A. Schmidt, eds. 2000. *Welfare and Work in the Open Economy.* Two volumes. Oxford: Oxford University Press.

Schuck, Peter H. and Richard J. Zeckhauser. 2006. *Targeting in Social Programs.* Washington, DC: Brookings Institution.

Scruggs, Lyle. 2004. "Welfare State Entitlements Data Set: A Comparative Institutional Analysis of Eighteen Welfare States." Data set. Version 1.0. <sp.uconn.edu/~scruggs/wp.htm>.

——James Allan. 2006. "The Material Consequences of Welfare States: Benefit Generosity and Absolute Poverty in 16 OECD Countries." *Comparative Political Studies* 39: 880–904.

Sefton, Tom, John Hills, and Holly Sutherland. 2009. "Poverty, Inequality, and Redistribution." Pp. 21–45 in *Towards a More Equal Society? Poverty, Inequality, and Policy since 1997*, edited by John Hills, Tom Sefton, and Kitty Stewart. Bristol, UK: Policy Press.

Sen, Amartya. 1976. "Poverty: An Ordinal Approach to Measurement." *Econometrica* 44: 219–31.

——1992. *Inequality Reexamined.* Cambridge, MA and New York: Harvard University Press and Russell Sage Foundation.

——1999. *Development as Freedom.* Oxford: Oxford University Press.

Shalev, Michael. 2007. "Limits and Alternatives to Multiple Regression in Comparative Research." *Comparative Social Research* 24: 261–308.

Shapiro, Robert Y. and John T. Young. 1989. "Public Opinion and the Welfare State: The United States in Comparative Perspective." *Political Science Quarterly* 104: 59–89.

Short, Kathleen S. 2005. "Material and Financial Hardship and Income-Based Poverty Measures in the USA." *Journal of Social Policy* 34: 21–38.

Sjöberg, Ola. 2010. "Social Insurance as a Collective Resource: Unemployment Benefits, Job Insecurity, and Subjective Well-Being in Comparative Perspective." *Social Forces* 88: 1281–304.

Skocpol, Theda. 1991. "Targeting within Universalism: Politically Viable Policies to Combat Poverty in the United States." Pp. 411–36 in *The Urban Underclass*, edited by Christopher Jencks and Paul E. Peterson. Washington, DC: Brookings Institution.

Slemrod, Joel and Jon Bakija. 2004. *Taxing Ourselves*. Third edition. Cambridge, MA: MIT Press.

Slesnick, Daniel T. 2001. *Consumption and Social Welfare*. Cambridge: Cambridge University Press.

Smeeding, Timothy M. 2005. "Public Policy, Economic Inequality, and Poverty: The United States in Comparative Perspective." *Social Science Quarterly* 86: 955–83.

——2006. "Poor People in Rich Nations: The United States in Comparative Perspective." *Journal of Economic Perspectives* 20(1): 69–90.

——Lee Rainwater, and Gary Burtless. 2001. "U.S. Poverty in a Cross-National Context." Pp. 162–89 in *Understanding Poverty*, edited by Sheldon H. Danziger and Robert H. Haveman. New York and Cambridge, MA: Russell Sage Foundation and Harvard University Press.

——Jane Waldfogel. 2010. "Fighting Poverty: Attentive Policy Can Make a Difference." *Journal of Policy Analysis and Management* 29: 401–7.

Snel, Erik, Jan de Boom, and Godfried Engbersen. 2008. "The Silent Transformation of the Dutch Welfare State and the Rise of In-Work Poverty." Pp. 124–54 in *The Working Poor in Europe*, edited by Hans-Jürgen Andreß and Henning Lohmann. Cheltenham, UK: Edward Elgar.

Steinmo, Sven. 1993. *Taxation and Democracy: Swedish, British, and American Approaches to Financing the Modern State*. New Haven, CT: Yale University Press.

Stiglitz, Joseph, Amartya Sen, and Jean-Paul Fitoussi. 2009. *Report by the Commission on the Measurement of Economic Performance and Social Progress*. <stiglitz-sen-fitoussi.fr>.

Streeck, Wolfgang. 2009. *Re-Forming Capitalism: Institutional Change in the German Political Economy*. Oxford: Oxford University Press.

Sullivan, James X., Leslie Turner, and Sheldon Danziger. 2008. "The Relationship between Income and Material Hardship." *Journal of Policy Analysis and Management* 27: 63–81.

Svallfors, Stefan. 1997. "Worlds of Welfare and Attitudes to Redistribution: A Comparison of Eight Western Nations." *European Sociological Review* 13: 283–304.

——, ed. 2007. *The Political Sociology of the Welfare State: Institutions, Social Cleavages, and Orientations*. Stanford, CA: Stanford University Press.

Tax Policy Center. 2010. "What Is the Earned Income Tax Credit." <taxpolicycenter.org/briefing-book/key-elements/family/eitc.cfm>.

Teitler, Julien O., Irwin Garfinkel, Sandra Garcia, and Susan Kenney. 2004. "New York City Social Indicators 2002." Social Indicators Survey Center. Columbia University School of Social Work.

Thompson, Gabriel. 2010. *Working in the Shadows: A Year of Doing the Jobs (Most) Americans Won't Do*. New York: Nation Books.

Titmuss, Richard M. 1973. *Social Policy: An Introduction*. Edited by Brian Abel-Smith and Kay Titmuss. New York: Pantheon.

Townsend, Peter. 1979. *Poverty in the United Kingdom: A Survey of Household Resources and Standards of Living*. Berkeley: University of California Press.

UNDP (United Nations Development Programme). 2007. *Human Development Report 2007/2008*. <hdr.undp.org/en/reports/global/hdr2007-8>.

UNRISD (United Nations Research Institute for Social Development). 2010. *Combating Poverty and Inequality*. <unrisd.org>.

U.S. Bureau of the Census. 2003. "Supplemental Measures of Material Well-Being: Expenditures, Consumption, and Poverty, 1998 and 2001." Current Population Reports P23-201. <census.gov/prod/2003pubs/p23-201.pdf>.

——2009. *Income, Poverty, and Health Insurance Coverage in the United States: 2008*. <census.gov/prod/2009pubs/p60-236.pdf>.

U.S. Department of Health and Human Services. 2004. "Measures of Material Hardship: Final Report." <aspe.hhs.gov/hsp/materialhardship04>.

van Dijk Jan, John van Nesteren, and Paul Smit. 2007. *Criminal Victimisation in International Perspective: Key Findings from the 2004–2005 ICVS and EU ICS*. Den Haag, Netherlands: Wetenschappelijk Onderzoeken Documentatiecentrum. <deventerkennisnet.nl/binaries/nicis/bulk/onderzoek/2008/2/3/icvs2004_05report.pdf>.

van Oorschot Wim. 2002. "Targeting Welfare: On the Functions and Dysfunctions of Means Testing in Social Policy." Pp. 171–93 in *World Poverty*, edited by Peter Townsend and David Gordon. Bristol, UK: The Policy Press.

Veenhoven, Ruut. 2010. *World Database of Happiness*. Erasmus University Rotterdam. <worlddatabaseofhappiness.eur.nl>.

Venn, Danielle. 2009. "Legislation, Collective Bargaining, and Enforcement: Updating the OECD Employment Protection Indicators." OECD Social, Employment, and Migration Working Paper 89. <oecd.org/els/workingpapers>.

Visser, Jelle. 2002. "The First Part-Time Economy in the World: A Model To Be Followed?" *Journal of European Social Policy* 12: 23–42.

——2006. "Union Membership Statistics in 24 Countries." *Monthly Labor Review*, January: 38–49.

——2009. "Institutional Characteristics of Trade Unions, Wage Setting, State Intervention and Social Pacts (ICTWSS)." Database. Amsterdam Institute for Advanced Labour Studies (AIAS). <uva-aias.net>.

——Anton Hemerijck. 1997. *A Dutch Miracle: Job Growth, Welfare Reform, and Corporatism in the Netherlands.* Amsterdam: Amsterdam University Press.

Waldfogel, Jane. 2006. *What Children Need.* Cambridge, MA: Harvard University Press.

——2010. *Britain's War on Poverty.* New York: Russell Sage Foundation.

Wallerstein, Michael. 1999. "Wage-Setting Institutions and Pay Inequality in Advanced Industrial Societies." *American Journal of Political Science* 43: 649–80.

Warren, Neil. 2008. "A Review of Studies on the Distributional Impact of Consumption Taxes in OECD Countries." OECD Social, Employment, and Migration Working Paper 64. <oecd.org/els/workingpapers>.

Weaver, R. Kent. 2009. "The Politics of Low-Income Families in the United States." Pp. 292–328 in *Making the Work-Based Safety Net Work Better,* edited by Carolyn J. Heinrich and John Karl Scholz. New York: Russell Sage Foundation.

Weir, Margaret and Theda Skocpol. 1985. "State Structures and the Possibilities for 'Keynesian' Responses to the Great Depression in Sweden, Britain, and the United States." Pp. 107–63 in *Bringing the State Back In,* edited by Peter Evans, Dietrich Rueschemeyer, and Theda Skocpol. Cambridge: Cambridge University Press.

Western, Bruce. 1996. "Vague Theory and Model Uncertainty in Macrosociology." *Sociological Methodology* 6: 165–92.

Whelan, Christopher T., Richard Layte, and Bertrand Maître. 2002. "Multiple Deprivation and Persistent Poverty in the European Union." *Journal of European Social Policy* 12: 91–105.

——2003. "Persistent Income Poverty and Deprivation in the European Union: An Analysis of the First Three Waves of the European Community Household Panel." *Journal of Social Policy* 32: 1–18.

——2004. "Understanding the Mismatch between Income Poverty and Deprivation: A Dynamic Comparative Analysis." *European Sociological Review* 20: 287–302.

——Brian Nolan. 2001. "Income, Deprivation, and Economic Strain: An Analysis of the European Community Panel." *European Sociological Review* 17: 357–72.

——Brian Nolan, and Bertrand Maître. 2007. "Consistent Poverty and Economic Vulnerability." Pp. 87–103 in *Best of Times? The Social Impact of the Celtic Tiger,* edited by Tony Fahey, Helen Russell, and Christopher T. Whelan. Dublin: Institute of Public Administration.

White, Stuart. 2004. "A Social Democratic Framework for Benefit Conditionality." in *Sanctions and Sweeteners: Rights and Responsibilities in the Benefits System*, edited by Kate Stanley and Liane Asta Lohde with Stuart White. London: Institute for Public Policy Research.

Whiteford, Peter. 2007. "Targeting, Redistribution, and Poverty Reduction in OECD Countries." Unpublished.

——2008. "How Much Redistribution Do Governments Achieve? The Role of Cash Transfers and Household Taxes." Chapter 4 in *Growing Unequal?* Paris: OECD.

——2009. "Transfer Issues and Directions for Reform: Australian Transfer Policy in Comparative Perspective." Unpublished. Social Policy Research Center, University of New South Wales.

——Willem Adema. 2008. "What Works Best in Reducing Child Poverty: A Benefit or Work Strategy?" OECD Social, Employment, and Migration Working Paper 51. <oecd.org/els/working-papers>.

Wilensky, Harold. 1975. *The Welfare State and Equality*. Berkeley: University of California Press.

——1976. *The New Corporatism, Centralization, and the Welfare State*. Beverly Hills, CA: Sage.

——2002. *Rich Democracies*. Berkeley: University of California Press.

World Bank. 2007. *Doing Business 2007*. <doingbusiness.org/documents/DoingBusiness2007_FullReport.pdf>.

World Economic Forum. 2008. *Global Competitiveness Report 2007–2008*. <weforum.org/pdf/Global_Competitiveness_Reports/Reports/gcr_2007/gcr2007_rankings.pdf>.

Wright, Erik Olin and Rachel Dwyer. 2003. "The Patterns of Job Expansions in the United States: A Comparison of the 1960s and 1990s." *Socio-Economic Review* 1: 289–325.

Young, Cristobal. 2009. "Model Uncertainty in Sociological Research: An Application to Religion and Economic Growth." *American Sociological Review* 74: 380–97.

Index

Note: page numbers in *italics* indicate tables and figures.